Bringing Race Back In

RACE, ETHNICITY, AND POLITICS

Luis Ricardo Fraga and Paula D. McClain, Editors

Bringing Race Back In

BLACK POLITICIANS, DERACIALIZATION, AND
VOTING BEHAVIOR IN THE AGE OF OBAMA

Christopher T. Stout

University of Virginia Press
CHARLOTTESVILLE AND LONDON

University of Virginia Press

© 2015 by the Rector and Visitors of the University of Virginia
Printed in the United States of America on acid-free paper

First published 2015

9 8 7 6 5 4 3 2 1

Library of Congress Cataloging-in-Publication Data

Stout, Christopher T., 1982–

   Bringing race back in : Black politicians, deracialization, and voting behavior in the age of Obama / Christopher T. Stout.

      pages   cm

   Includes bibliographical references and index.

   ISBN 978-0-8139-3668-0 (cloth : acid-free paper) — ISBN 978-0-8139-3669-7 (e-book)

    1. African Americans—Politics and government—21st century. 2. African American politicians. 3. Political candidates—United States. 4. Race—Political aspects—United States. 5. Voting—United States. 6. Political participation—Unites States. 7. United States—Race relations—Political aspects. 8. United States—Politics and government—2009– I. Title.

   E185.615.S758 2014

   323.1196'073—dc23

2014020593

This book is dedicated to my family
Theresa Stout, Timothy Stout, and Vanessa Stout
And my wife
Kelsy Kretschmer

Contents

Acknowledgments

While this book project may appear in some ways to be a solo venture, it is really the product of a collective effort. As such, this book would not have been possible without the hard work and support of my advisors, colleagues, and friends.

The idea and plan for this book is born out of the guidance that I received from the faculty at the University of California, Irvine. In particular, I would like to thank Katherine Tate not only for helping me develop and explore the research questions in this book but also for all of her support and advice throughout the process. I would also like to thank Louis DeSipio, whose devotion to the education and success of his students is truly inspirational. Louis played an invaluable role in helping me refine and shape the theory in this book. I would also like to thank Carole Uhlaner and Bernie Grofman, who were instrumental in the development and design of this research project.

I would like to express gratitude for the comments and conversations about the book from all of my colleagues at University of California, Irvine, Wellesley College, and Southern Illinois University, Carbondale, friends, and other scholars including Steven Boutcher, Steve Bloom, Randy Burnside, Tom Burke, Kris Coulter, Randy Davis, Jennifer Garcia, Stacie Goddard, Tobin Grant, Laura Grattan, Benjamin Lind, Danvy Le, Phillip Habel, John Hamman, Hahrie Han, Laura Hatcher, Dante Jackson, David Jackson, Nick Jackson, Marion Just, Reuben Kline, Gregory Leslie, Natalie Masuoka, Mara Marks, Scott McClurg, Peter Miller, Kathy Rim, Nancy Scherer, Kim Shella, Fred Solt and Grace Stout. My colleagues and friends provided me with both the support and critical insights necessary to advance the work presented in this book.

I also am eternally grateful for the research assistance of Megan Garratt-Reed, Shane Gleason, Maja Wright-Phillips, and Srobana Bhattacharya. These scholars were vital in helping me collect and analyze data, and their comments and suggestions influenced the structure of the book. Their involvement with the project helped me produce a much better text. I am particularly appreciative of the help that Megan Garratt-Reed provided in the early stages. Without her assistance with content coding, I would not have been able to complete this project.

The editors and staff at the University of Virginia Press have been incredible throughout this process. For that reason, I would like to thank the University of Virginia Press editors for the series on race and ethnicity in urban politics, Paula McClain and Luis Fraga. I would also like to express my gratitude to Dick Holway, who was always willing to counsel me and provide advice not only on the process of writing a book but also on ways to improve its content. The Press editors and staff have made this experience easier and much more pleasurable than I had expected.

I was also fortunate to find Paula Maute at Word Wise editing. Her initial copyediting was extremely important in clarifying the messages presented in this book.

I would also like to thank Martin Johnson. Without his guidance when I was an undergraduate at the University of California, Riverside, I would not have been in the position to write this book. His dedication to mentoring undergraduates is something that I try to emulate every day. I am also greatful for Paula McClain and the Ralph Bunche Summer Institute, which prepared me well for graduate school and introduced me to many of the topics that are covered in this book.

My wife, Kelsy Kretschmer, deserves special recognition for her help. My work and my life have become infinitely better since the beginning of our relationship. This project would still be in its nascent stages without her counsel and support. Kelsy assisted me in developing the theory for this project and coached me through every mini-crisis that I encountered. I am forever in her debt for all of her love and guidance.

Finally, I am deeply appreciative of my parents, Timothy and Theresa Stout, and my sister, Vanessa Stout. The political discussions in my household were the impetus for my interest in politics. In addition to inspiring my passion for political science, they provided me with all the resources necessary for success, including always being willing to discuss some of the more mundane aspects of this book. My family's love and support were invaluable in my work. For this reason, this book is dedicated to them.

Bringing Race Back In

Introduction

In a February 2012 interview with *Ebony* magazine, African American actor Samuel L. Jackson proffered a theory on black political behavior: "I voted for Barack because he was black [and] that's why other folks vote for other people, because they look like them. . . . That's American politics, pure and simple. [Obama's] message didn't mean [anything] to me."[1] While the comment was impetuous, the essence of the statement rings true for many political pundits and politicians: black voters are much more likely to support a black candidate than a white candidate, regardless of the candidate's message or political affiliation.

Historically, the assumption that black voters will unanimously support black candidates has been reflected in exit polls and election results. The mechanism that explained this relationship was also clear, as black voters and candidates shared similar policy objectives. Moreover, black candidates have traditionally devoted a significant amount of effort and resources appealing to black voters. For example, 1972 presidential candidate Shirley Chisholm embraced the black community in her campaign. In a speech she noted that she was "black and proud."[2] In 1984, Democratic presidential candidate Jesse Jackson explicitly proclaimed that one of the primary goals of his candidacy would be to mobilize minority voters.[3] In cities like Chicago and Memphis, black mayoral candidates appealed to blacks using slogans like "It's our turn" and "Our time has come." Congressional representatives from Adam Clayton Powell (D-NY, 1945–71) to Maxine Waters (D-CA, 1991–present) routinely advocated for a progressive racial agenda and chastised the government for not doing enough to alleviate the economic and social plight of black Americans.

Today, in many ways, black voters and black candidates no longer share the same connection. While the majority of black voters still prefer racial policies such as affirmative action, more black candidates are ignoring or even opposing race-based legislation.[4] Moreover, black candidates in recent campaigns have been minimizing their associations with the black community. Twenty-four years after Jesse Jackson's 1984 presidential bid, Barack Obama, a first-term U.S. senator from Illinois, announced his presidential candidacy, but in contrast with Jackson's announcement, he did not explicitly mention race. While Jackson focused on empowering and mobilizing blacks, Obama's speech focused on bipartisanship and ending the wars in Iraq and Afghanistan.

The absence of racial appeals has not been uncommon recently for black candidates who seek elected offices in majority white settings.[5] Douglas Wilder, the first African American to be elected governor in the United States (D-VA, 1990–94), argued that in order to garner white support, "the black candidate's job is to prepare and position himself in such a way as to make race less of a factor."[6] If the black vote is static, as actor Samuel L. Jackson suggests, it is only rational that black candidates focus their efforts on appealing to white voters, who are often skeptical of black candidates, rather than devoting their resources to black voters whose support is near certain.[7] This is why black U.S. Senate and gubernatorial candidates, from Senator Edward W. Brooke III (R-MA, 1966–78) to Governor Deval L. Patrick (D-MA, 2006–present) haven't insisted that it is our turn or that blacks need to be represented by other blacks. Instead, their lack of focus on race-based topics leads many voters (black and white) to see these black candidates as no different from their white counterparts. Mike Hurley, the white owner of the *Boston Minuteman Press,* notes, "I don't even see Deval Patrick as black."[8] This deracialized style of campaigning may improve black candidates' standing with white voters, but contrary to Samuel L. Jackson's assertion, it may not allow them to attract black support in the same way as black candidates who routinely make racial appeals.

The precipitous growth in the number of black U.S. Senate and gubernatorial candidates in recent years, President Obama's success in 2008 and 2012, and the deracialized campaign styles that are becoming increasingly common among black candidates raise several timely questions about political behavior and race in the twenty-first century. In particular, are deracialized campaigns as effective in mobilizing and garnering support from black voters as racialized campaigns? Is deracialized campaigning necessary for today's black politicians, or can black candidates make specific appeals to the black community without sacrificing white and Latino support? Finally, if black voters favor black candidates who highlight race in their campaigns, what explains this preference?

Previous studies on deracialization provide important insights into the relationship between race-neutral campaign styles and voting behavior; however, the inconclusive and often conflicting nature of the results suggest that more research is necessary. In particular, more work needs to be done to explore whether some types of racial appeals are more electorally advantageous than a deracialized campaign strategy. While previous measures of racial appeals take into account the varying degrees of racialization, examine differences between implicit and explicit racial appeals, and use a multidimensional approach to measure this campaign style, they do not differentiate between constructive racial appeals and racially divisive appeals.[9]

This book improves our understanding of the efficacy of racialized campaigns by disaggregating positive racial appeals that demonstrate that the candidate will either advance black policy interests or highlight the candidate's connection to the black community *without attacking outside political players* and negative racial appeals that attack a political opponent, the media, or a supposed ally in a racially divisive manner in hopes of conjuring up support from black voters. It is important to disaggregate and measure these two forms of racial appeals separately because black candidates who racialize often use both negative and positive racial appeals. If one type of appeal has a positive effect on the electorate, and the other has a negative effect, measuring both on the same scale will produce misleading results. By disaggregating these two types of racial appeals, we gain a more comprehensive overview about whether black candidates can ever appeal to the black community without sacrificing white or Latino support. These more nuanced racialization measures also allow us to better understand whether the tone of racial appeals matters in how voters assess black candidates.

Second, most previous work on racialization tends to focus on the influence of racial appeals made by white candidates on the electorate as a whole. This work complements previous research by examining the influence of racial appeals made by black candidates and by examining the unique effect these appeals have on blacks, whites, and Latinos *separately*. For the former, the substantial increase in the number of black candidates campaigning for elected office in majority white settings increases the need to understand how these candidates' use of, or abstinence from, racial appeals influences their likelihood of success. Given that black politicians are often perceived as having different strengths and weaknesses than white candidates, it would not be surprising to find that racial appeals made by black candidates are judged differently.

It is important to examine the effect of race-based appeals on the various racial/ethnic groups separately given their distinctive outlooks on politics. For example, it seems likely that minority voters, and in particular blacks, may find racial appeals as being more persuasive than their white counterparts. As a result, it is probable that an individual's race will influence whether they reward or punish black candidates for making race-based appeals. By examining the relationship between black candidates' use of racial appeals and these appeals' distinct influence on different racial/ethnic groups, we gain a broader understanding of the advantages and disadvantages of race-based appeals.

Finally, this book builds on previous research on racialization by examining the influence of positive and negative racial appeals using both a large sample of high-profile statewide black candidates and by performing in-depth case studies of two prominent black presidential candidates. Most previous research that explores the efficacy of racial appeals focuses on case studies of one or two elections at one point in time. These studies provide vital information about the connection between black candidates' campaign styles and political behavior, but leave room for improvement. By examining only one or two cases in isolation, previous research cannot show the *average effect* that a deracialized campaign style has on voter turnout and electoral support over a broader set of cases. This small case research design is also unable to demonstrate that racial appeals have any influence on the electorate when accounting for other factors such as the candidate's political partisanship and/or viability.

To account for this problem this study utilizes information about thirty-three black U.S. Senate and gubernatorial candidates who campaigned for high-profile statewide office between 1982 and 2010 to examine how the electorate responds to different racial campaign styles. These campaigns, along with state exit poll data and U.S. Census information, provide a broader overview of the efficacy of deracialized and racialized campaigns in influencing voter turnout and electoral support.

In addition to exploring the relationship between deracialized campaigns and electoral behavior with a large set of minority candidates, this study also uses in-depth case studies of the presidential campaigns of Barack Obama and Jesse Jackson to better understand the intermediating mechanisms between racial appeals and voting behavior. The analysis of their campaigns also allows me to assess whether levels of support for these candidates changes during the same election cycle after highly publicized racial appeals. This exercise provides the opportunity to better explore whether racialized campaign strategies have any causal influence on political behavior. By examining a larger sample of black candidates in various contexts simultaneously and performing in-depth case studies of black presidential candidates, this study is better able to isolate the connection between black candidates' use of race-based appeals and voting behavior than previous studies.

In this introduction, I define deracialization and review literature on the efficacy of positive and negative racial appeals in mobilizing and winning votes from different racial and ethnic groups. I then discuss the need for a more comprehensive study of this relationship using comparisons of different black candidates. Following this discussion, I outline more detailed definitions of racial appeals and discuss how these measures are content coded in this study.

What Is Deracialization, and Does It Work?

Charles V. Hamilton, one of the co-authors of *Black Power* (1968), presented one of the earliest discussions of a deracialized campaign strategy in a 1977 article. Confronting a conservative backlash from the civil rights movement, Hamilton (1977) recognized that the Republican Party was using the Democratic Party's racial platform to attract white voters. To combat growing white disillusionment with the Democratic Party, Hamilton suggested that black candidates and the Democratic Party in general should advocate for issues which transcend race to broaden their appeal to a more diverse electorate.[10]

In the coming years, political scientists would further analyze and refine what it meant to run a campaign that was devoid of race-based appeals. In the 1993 study "The Conceptualization of Deracialization," McCormick and Jones describe deracialized campaigns as those "conducted in a stylistic fashion that defuse the polarizing effects of race by avoiding explicit reference to race-specific issues, while at the same time emphasizing those issues which are racially transcendent" (76). In addition to minimizing discussions of race-based issues, McCormick and Jones suggest that deracialized campaigns should avoid public appeals to blacks to minimize the risk of alienating white and Latino voters. In sum, by avoiding race-based appeals, candidates aim to demonstrate their independence from the black community.

In the previous two decades, an increasing number of black candidates running in majority white districts have been utilizing a deracialized campaign strategy.[11] For blacks to be elected or promoted to leadership positions in state and national government, it is hypothesized that they have to appeal to the racial majority, whether it be black, white, or Latino.[12] In essence, the deracialized campaign style is considered a pragmatic tactic that black candidates use when running in majority white settings.[13] Moreover, based on the assumption that black voters will automatically vote for black politicians, many black candidates do not devote their limited resources to appeal to co-racial voters, particularly if racial appeals are assumed to diminish support among whites and Latinos. However in spite of the growing numbers of deracialized campaigns in recent years, the efficacy of a race-neutral strategy continues to be debated.

In separate studies of high-profile black candidates running for statewide offices, Jeffries (1999), Strickland and Whicker (1992), Sonenshein (1990),

Jones and Clemons (1993), and Frederick and Jeffries (2009) find that the most successful black candidates avoid making race-based appeals. According to Summers and Klinkner (1991), the deracialization hypothesis posits that white voters "will accept a black candidate who talks like the average white politician" (203). For example, the deracialized campaign style of black North Carolina U.S. Senate candidate Harvey Gantt in 1990 led one white North Carolinian to note, "Your man is lookin' whiter and whiter every day; there must be no more than 20 [blacks] in this whole county, and Gantt's gonna get two-thirds of the whole vote."[14] This finding is not isolated. In a study of former Los Angeles mayor Tom Bradley's 1982 gubernatorial campaign in California, Citrin et al. (1990) find that Bradley's nonracial style minimized voters' tendency to vote along racial lines. In addition to minimizing perceived racial differences, a deracialized campaign style is hypothesized to be effective because it demonstrates that the black candidate will not favor black voters, which can be particularly damaging for those campaigning in a majority white setting.[15]

Recent research demonstrates that black voters also respond positively to black candidates who abstain from making race-based appeals. In an interview with historian William Jelani Cobb (2010), former Southern Christian Leadership Council president Joseph Lowery notes that black voters are hesitant to support black candidates without cross-racial appeal. "Black folks have already had a symbolic candidate with Jesse in 1988, and they did not want to throw away a vote on more symbolism. Barack Obama had to prove that he could actually win white votes before he could count on black ones (9)." Lowery's quote demonstrates that black voters prefer viable black candidates to those whose racialized platforms decrease their electability.

Along these lines, Tate (2012) argues that as blacks incorporate into the polity, a greater percentage of them display a preference for racially moderate black candidates. This preference is explained by black voters' rejection of a racially confrontational style, which appears to limit blacks' opportunities in electoral politics, in favor of a racially cooperative strategy. McIlwain and Caliendo (2011) agree that blacks have limited tolerance for race-based appeals in a "post-racial" society. In sum, research demonstrates that black candidates perform better among both whites and blacks if they take a more moderate tone on racial issues and minimize their associations with the black community.

However, other research indicates that complete abstinence from race-based appeals can sabotage a black candidate's bid for elected office. A growing body of literature finds that deracialized campaigns lead to higher levels of apathy among minority voters.[16] Given that many black elected officials' success is contingent on their ability to build a coalition between a highly mobilized group of minorities and liberal whites, a lack of enthusiasm in the black community can be disastrous. While Citrin et al. (1990) note that Tom Bradley's 1982 deracialized gubernatorial campaign style increased his support among white voters in California, they argue that it also led to lower levels of black turnout at the polls, which could have made the difference in an election where Bradley's opponent, *George Deukmejian*, won by less than 2 percent.

Similarly, Orey (2006) found that when Jackson, Mississippi, mayoral candidate Harvey Johnson ignored issues important to blacks in 1993, he did not mobilize co-racial voters and lost as a result. However, in Johnson's successful second run for mayor in 1997, he appealed to the black community and black turnout increased significantly. Most recently, black candidate Artur Davis, a four-term U.S. representative from Alabama, ran a deracialized campaign in the 2010 Democratic primary for governor, but failed due in part to lackluster support from African Americans. As *Newsweek* contributor Ellis Cose noted, "Davis's spectacular collapse makes abundantly clear that, even in the age of Obama, black politicians can easily wander into quicksand as they try to move beyond their traditional black base."[17] Candidates such as Davis, who abstain from making racial appeals, may alienate black voters and, as a result, lose their support.

Beyond the deracialization tactic's lack of efficacy in mobilizing black voters, some research questions whether deracialized campaigns even improve black candidates' standing with white voters. Former Atlanta mayor and U.S. congressman Andrew Young, for example, failed in his Democratic primary gubernatorial bid in Georgia in 1990 because of his deracialized campaign's inability to both mobilize the black community and draw the support of white voters.[18] Similarly, Obama ran what many describe a deracialized campaign in 2012.[19] In spite of attempting to appeal to a broader electorate, Obama received less than 40 percent of the white vote in the 2012 presidential election.

While previous research has provided much information about the influence of racial appeals on the electorate, the conflicting results for the efficacy of race-based appeals indicates that more research is necessary. In particular, we may gain more leverage on these opposing findings if we disaggregate racial appeals by their tone. Given that racialized black candidates often use both positive and negative racial appeals, it is possible that one form of racialization has a positive effect that may be drowned out or counterbalanced by the opposite type of racial appeal. Thus the differences in the aforementioned studies may be due to the balance of racial appeals of different tones.

For example, lumping black candidates who predominately use positive racial appeals with those who predominately use negative racial appeals under the same racialized "umbrella" may create a flawed comparison of racialized and deracialized candidates. This may account for the conflicting findings detailed above. However, by disaggregating racial appeals by their tone, we may gain a better understanding of which, if any, racialized campaigns are preferable to a deracialized approach.

Positive and Negative Forms of Racialization

The racialization measures used in this study differentiates between positive and negative forms of racial appeals. For instance, when a black candidate speaks at a black church or advocates for greater levels of racial diversity in public institutions, he or she is making a positive racial appeal, and when a black candidate blames racism for their lack of support or attacks an opponent for injecting race into the campaign, he or she is making a negative racial appeal. While both forms of racial appeals have the same goal of drawing black votes, they reach out to voters in very different ways and carry different levels of risks and rewards. With these measures, we can better examine if these two types of racial appeals garner support from, make no difference to, or alienate black, white, and Latino voters.

Positive Racial Appeals

Positive racial appeals demonstrate that the candidate will either advance black policy interests or highlight the candidate's connection to the black community *without attacking outside political players or institutions.* Thus, positive racial appeals allow black candidates to improve their standing in the black community in two ways. First, those who racialize in a positive manner may enjoy higher levels of support because they can demonstrate their intentions of advancing black political interests.

In spite of growing black representation in government in recent decades, large disparities between blacks and whites in everything from wealth, life expectancy, and educational attainment continue to exist. Black candidates who show that they are interested in addressing these racial deficits may be in a better position to attract black support. Consistent with this idea, Ansolabehere and Jones (2010) demonstrate that voters punish and reward elected officials based on whether their voting record in Congress is closer to or farther from their own preferences. The same holds true for African Americans. Glaser (1988) demonstrates that Mississippi congressman Bennie Thompson performed better among blacks than his deracialized black predecessor, Mike Espy, because Thompson unapologetically discussed how he would focus on advancing black political interests. Similarly, a recent survey showed that African Americans who believe Obama has done more for the black community than previous presidents are three times more likely to approve of his performance.[20] When black politicians are perceived as working for black political interests, they are often rewarded with greater levels of black support.

Conversely, black elected officials who oppose policies that most black voters support often face a backlash. Alabama Democratic congressman Artur Davis's vote against the Affordable Care Act drew condemnation from many black elites. Jesse Jackson, for example, criticized Davis's vote by noting, "You can't vote against healthcare and call yourself a black man."[21] Jackson's comment insinuates that black elected officials who do not represent black interests are violating the norms of racial solidarity in the black community. Davis's lack of policy congruence with co-racial voters appeared to damage his reputation with blacks in his state. As mentioned earlier, Davis failed in his bid to become the Alabama Democratic gubernatorial nominee in 2010 due to lackluster support from black voters.

Blacks may also be more inspired to participate in politics when a candidate discusses issues that are salient in the black community. For example, Harold Washington's 1983 campaign for mayor of Chicago inspired high levels of black turnout that many attribute to his campaign's focus on issues which were important to blacks in the city (Preston 1983). Los Angeles mayor Tom Bradley, on the other hand, saw declining levels of black turnout over time when he was on the ballot. Gilliam and Kaufmann (1998) argue that this decline in turnout is due to a disempowerment effect that was predicated on frustrations with Bradley's inattention to the black community. Taken together, it is possible that black voters will be the most enthusiastic and supportive of candidates who make racial appeals demonstrating that they will advance black policy interests.

Second, positive racial appeals may appeal to black voters through a sense of shared experiences and racial camaraderie. When black candidates make positive racial appeals through appearances at antipoverty forums and at black church services or give interviews to media organizations that draw overwhelming black audiences, they signal concern for the black community and highlight their association with other African Americans. A number of studies demonstrate that voters generally respond well to politicians who appear to understand their needs.[22] In his 2003 ethnographic study of black U.S. House representatives, Fenno showed that black voters responded well to black elected officials who were perceived as working hard for their interests and as being empathetic with the black experience. Fenno recounts Ohio black congressman Louis Stokes's introduction at a gathering organized by a black sorority in which the congressman was described as "a man who has known poverty and overcome it, a man who knows what it is to be part of an oppressed people—our people" (36). Fenno noted that Stokes's connection with the black community was so strong that he was treated like a celebrity and was seen as a trusted voice in the black community. "He is a qualified leader, respected, admired, and trusted without hesitation. His black constituents are not cynical or suspicious. After the talk he was mobbed by these mature, adult, college-educated black women—for his *autograph*. I never saw that before" (36). Fenno's discussion of Stokes demonstrates that when black elected officials are perceived as working for black interests, they enjoy high levels of support. Thus candidates who make positive racial appeals by speaking at black organizations, as Stokes did, should enjoy higher levels of trust, support, and enthusiasm from the black community.

Conversely, when black candidates distance themselves from the black community, it can lead some African Americans to question whether their connection to the nominee is purely superficial.[23] In the 2002 Newark, New Jersey, mayoral election, a number of blacks voted against deracialized black candidate Cory Booker because of concerns that he was not "black enough."[24] Black candidates who de-emphasize their connection to the black community by refraining from making positive racial appeals may be perceived as unconcerned about African Americans and the obstacles they face. As a result, a significant segment of the black community may be less enthusiastic about supporting "post-racial" candidates.

Deracialized candidates may also be perceived as exploiting the black vote for their own political gain. In the 2002 Newark mayoral election, black incumbent mayor Sharpe James accused deracialized black candidate Cory Booker of using the majority black city as an experiment to build up his credentials to run for a higher office.[25] Illinois congressman Bobby Rush made similar claims against Barack Obama in a 2000 congressional election. Both cases indicate that black candidates who try to distance themselves from the black community are vulnerable to claims that they are opportunistic and do not have a genuine interest in improving the lives of African Americans.[26] However, the use of positive racial appeals may help blunt such criticism.

Similarly, whites may not punish black candidates who utilize positive race-based appeals. In her 1993 study of black congressional representatives, Swain finds that many white voters would support even racially progressive black candidates. Along these lines, there is some evidence that white voters, and liberals in particular, will actually be more supportive of black candidates who focus on improving conditions in the black community or highlighting their association with co-racial voters. Minnesota congressman Keith Ellison, for example, is said to have increased his support in nonblack communities because of his liberal platform and racial background.[27] Sniderman and Stiglitz (2008) find that some whites who held blacks in high-esteem were more supportive of Obama because of his race. Thus it is possible that black candidates may lose some segment of white voters when engaging in race-based appeals, but may counterbalance these losses with gains among white liberals. In combination, black candidates who use positive race-based appeals may ultimately not experience large differences in white support compared with their "post-racial" counterparts.

Positive racial appeals are not without their shortcomings. The greatest risk is that they increase fears that black candidates will engage in racial favoritism.[28] The strength of a deracialized campaign is that it minimizes concerns among white and Latino voters that black candidates will govern any differently than their white counterparts. However, black candidates who engage in race-based appeals may increase fears that black candidates will pay more attention to their racial group at the expense of nonblacks. A number of studies demonstrate that black candidates who are perceived as favoring blacks over others receive significantly lower levels of white and Latino support.[29] As a result, positive racial appeals may increase black candidates' support among co-racial voters at the cost of the white and Latino vote.

Moreover, black candidates who champion issues that are explicitly or implicitly tied to the black community are also more susceptible to race-based attacks from their opponents. In 1990, Democratic North Carolina U.S. Senate candidate Harvey Gantt's support for affirmative action was used against him in a campaign commercial by his opponent, Jesse Helms, the Republican five-term North Carolina senator. Along the same lines, white candidate Richard Williamson attacked his black opponent, Carol Moseley Braun, for being weak on crime in the 1992 Illinois U.S. Senate campaign season because, among other things, she opposed the death penalty. In a commercial, Williamson's campaign noted, "While crime and violence grip our streets, Carol Moseley Braun opposes the death penalty and wants to decriminalize marijuana."[30] The advertisement played on whites' fears that black candidates will be too soft on crime and conjures up negative attitudes about blacks as criminals. These types of attacks have been shown to increase doubts about black candidates and diminish their support, particularly from white voters.[31]

Negative Racial Appeals

Negative racial appeals attempt to mobilize black voters by highlighting racism in society. These appeals are generally devoid of any substantive policy proposals and usually take the form of an attack on a political opponent, the media, or a supposed ally. Negative racial appeals demonstrate a connection to the black community by reminding black voters that their economic and political opportunities, like the candidates themselves, are limited by racism in society. Negative racial appeals may be effective because they rouse feelings of frustration among blacks. In turn, this frustration may inspire blacks to rally around the black candidate's campaign. In essence, negative racial appeals use the idea of racial solidarity and claims of racism to increase support among sympathetic voters.

In addition to drawing black votes, negative racial appeals also may damage the reputations of black politicians' political rivals. Given that most Americans reject overt racism, negative racial appeals may be effective because they lead people to be less supportive of candidates or political entities who are perceived as treating people unfairly because of their race.

Negative racial appeals may be an effective tool black candidates can use to shake up faltering campaigns or alter the narrative in contexts where the black candidate is receiving low levels of support. For example, a black candidate may accuse the opposing party or the media of not treating him fairly because of his race. Through political pressure from those who are sympathetic to calls of racism, this appeal may change the nature of support or coverage the candidate receives from different political entities. In summary, negative racial appeals have the potential to draw support from sympathetic voters while damaging the reputation of adversaries.

While less common than positive racial appeals, negative racial appeals are not anomalies in American politics. For example, when former D.C. mayor Marion Barry was arrested for soliciting, buying, and using cocaine, many of those close to Barry engaged in a negative racial appeal by arguing that the FBI sting was a conspiracy to bring down black politicians. The comment was meant to absolve Barry of his crimes and to court support for those who might be sympathetic to claims of racism in law enforcement. Moreover, the negative racial appeal also was meant to delegitimize the FBI's investigation for unfairly targeting Barry due to his race.

A similar example of a negative racial appeal is when Clarence Thomas argued that sexual harassment charges from a former employee, Anita Hill, and the media's perpetuation of the scandal were a high-tech lynching meant to thwart his nomination for the Supreme Court.[32] Several scholars noted that Thomas's comments to the judiciary committee were effective in drawing black support and moving his confirmation forward.[33] Stanford law professor Richard Thompson Ford noted that Thomas's appeal was effective because "even those disinclined to support Thomas on his merits might worry that the stereotype of the oversexed black man colored, so to speak, the proceedings."[34] Most recently, a super PAC representing 2012 black presidential candidate Herman Cain argued that sexual harassment charges against Cain were also a form of high-tech lynching by liberals and the media.

While negative racial appeals may improve black candidates' standing in the electorate, they are fraught with potential pitfalls. Namely, research demonstrates that voters do not always perceive claims of racism as credible. In fact, Nelson, Sanbonmatsu, and McClerking (2007) demonstrate that claims of racism by black candidates and especially black liberals are more likely to be perceived as an insincere ploy rather than a true grievance. Ford (2008) argues that for these reasons black elected officials/candidates often face a backlash from voters for engaging in what some see as unnecessary or frivolous claims of racism.

Moreover, voters may reject negative racial appeals because they discuss racism in a "post-racial" society. A number of studies demonstrate that voters of all races/ethnicities reject race-baiting.[35] Moreover, voters may punish black candidates for arguing that race continues to be a barrier in an America that has elected its first black president. African American Reverend Eugene Rivers of Azusa Christian Community Church noted in the 2008 election that Obama was "taking the black community to a new level of understanding and responsibility. No longer are we going to trade in the politics of grievance."[36] Rivers comments insinuates that voters, and even some black voters, may be unsupportive of black candidates who argue that racism still is a limiting factor in American politics in the age of Obama.

Negative racial appeals may also be particularly offensive to white voters, some of whom fear "reverse racism." In the *Audacity of Hope*, Obama writes, "Even the most fair-minded of Whites, those who would genuinely like to see racial inequality ended and poverty relieved tend to push back against suggestions of racial victimization."[37] While voters may believe that racism is still a problem, they may punish black politicians who discuss race in a confrontational manner. As a result, those who inject race into the campaign in a divisive fashion could lose support from voters of all races and particularly among whites.

Measuring Racialization

While most scholars can agree on the definition of a racialized campaign and can identify candidates who utilize these strategies, it is difficult to quantify this campaign style for purposes of comparison. Metz and Tate (1995) describe measuring racialization as former Supreme Court Associate Justice Stewart Potter described pornography. It's difficult to explain, but most people can recognize it when they see it. The lack of a systematic measure for racialization has generally not been a problem for scholars as most studies on this topic center on a single case. A study of a larger set of cases, however, requires a systematic measure of racial appeals.

Despite the difficulty in measuring racialization, social scientists use a number of innovative techniques to evaluate this seemingly amorphous concept, including surveying black candidates to better understand their racial campaign strategy and measuring the racial makeup of the audiences at campaign events.[38] Metz and Tate (1995) conduct content analysis of newspaper articles and create a twelve-point additive scale that accounts for differences in black candidates' racial rhetoric (e.g., whether they refer to African American issues, or use terms like *racism, injustice,* or *social justice*), the issues they support, and their campaign appearances (e.g., the frequency of their appearances in predominately black neighborhoods and venues like black churches). McIlwain and Caliendo (2011) take a similar approach and evaluate racialization through content analysis of campaign television commercials. To measure racialization they use a scale of more than fifty ways in which black candidates can appeal to black voters, which range from racial imagery, racial stereotypes, and political issues.

Similar to many studies that have assessed levels of racialization, I conducted content analysis of newspaper articles covering black candidates who campaigned for the U.S. Senate or governor between 1982 and 2010.[39] I limited my study to these high-profile statewide offices because information about these candidates is available regardless of their performance. Moreover, the high-profile nature of their candidacies increases the likelihood that voters will have heard of the candidate's racial platform.

To conduct this analysis, I start with black candidates who ran against a nonblack candidate for U.S. Senate or governor between 1982 and 2010.[40] I searched for each candidate's name in LexisNexis and Access World News for all dates between September 1 and Election Day of that year. I then took a random sample of seventy-five articles on each campaign, and I excluded candidates with fewer than forty articles during these two months.[41] In total, the data set includes over 2,200 newspaper articles with the coverage of thirty-three biracial elections with a black gubernatorial or U.S. Senate candidate.

I used newspapers for statewide candidates more than broadcast (TV and radio) and online news sources for several reasons.[42] First, research shows a high correlation between the content of newspaper coverage and other media outlets' coverage.[43] Thus my results should not be heavily skewed by my selection of newspaper articles over other forms of media. Second, newspapers provide a broader view of the campaign than most television news reports and candidate websites. In particular, newspapers include more detailed coverage about candidate appearances, candidates' and campaign officials' statements, and campaign controversies or gaffes than candidate websites and some broadcast media.[44] Third, research has shown that print media plays a powerful role in shaping individuals' attitudes about candidates, policies, and political parties.[45] Fourth, information in newspapers is readily available over time, unlike online blogs and television news coverage that are not easily accessible or *do not cover all races* over the period (1982–2010). For the sake of consistency, I focus my attention on print media. Finally, several highly regarded studies have used newspaper coverage to assess racialization.[46]

This study's unit of analysis is the newspaper article, rather than the total number of paragraphs in each article. My coding scheme is based on the work of McIlwain and Caliendo (2011) and Metz and Tate (1995), who provide detailed summaries of how they code political commercials and newspaper articles for racial content. Similar to these studies, I code each article on four attributes: Issues, Audience, Racially Coded Language, and Associations. Within each article, I collect information about the black candidate's use of implicit positive, explicit positive, and negative racial appeals. Only comments or actions taken by the candidates or significant players in their campaigns (campaign manager, press secretary, and chairman) are coded. Thus comments made by lower-level staff workers, the National Democratic or Republican Party, or an individual who did not play an integral role in the campaign or its strategy are excluded from this measure.[47]

For each article, I gave a score of 0 to 2 for the positive racialization measure and a score of 0 or 1 for the negative racialization measure. For both racialization measures, 0 signifies that race is not mentioned in the article. For the positive racialization measure, a score of 1 indicates implicit or weak associations with race, and a score of 2 indicates that the candidate mentioned race explicitly or made strong connections to their race or racial topics. Given that all negative racial appeals are explicit, a score of 1 on the negative racialization measure indicates that the candidate made a negative racial appeal in the article. The maximum score that an article can receive is 2 for the positive racialization measure and 1 for the negative racialization measure, regardless of how many times race is mentioned in the article.[48] After coding the set of articles for each candidate, I averaged the positive and negative racialization scores across all of the articles and assigned this score to the candidate. The coding scheme was designed to minimize coder bias. Intercoder reliability assessments showed that this approach was successful.[49] Below is a more detailed summary of the coding system.[50]

Positive Racial Appeals

ISSUES

A newspaper article received a positive racialization score of 0 if the issues addressed by the candidate in the article had no historical association with race, racism, or racial divisions including the candidate's position on the economy, tax cuts, the environment, campaign finance reform, infrastructure, gay rights, gun rights, gambling, education, or the military. A newspaper article was given a score of 1 if the newspaper article focused on issues that could be tangentially associated with race. For example, if the candidate expressed a liberal position on crime, welfare, felon disenfranchisement, unemployment, increasing investments in poor neighborhoods or schools, capital punishment, increases in minimum wage, immigration, or drugs, they were given a score of 1.[51] All of these issues greatly impact the black community, but by themselves they are not explicitly racial. Moreover, many of these issues have been used to examine the impact of implicit racial appeals on political behavior.[52] Finally, articles were given a score of 2 if the candidate was reported to advocate or support issues explicitly tied to race. For example, those who supported affirmative action policies, increased funding for African foreign aid, civil rights legislation, school busing, or any race-based policy received a score of 2. Moreover, the newspaper article received a score of 2 if the candidate associated their support of certain government actions or policies with minority interests. In 2002, Dallas mayor Ron Kirk, in campaigning for a Texas U.S. Senate seat, said he was wary of supporting the war in Iraq because minorities would be disproportionately on the front lines.[53] While opposing the war does not inject race into the campaign, connecting it to minority interests does so explicitly. Table 1 summarizes how the different issues were coded.

AUDIENCE

Where candidates speak can reveal as much about them as *what they say.*[54] Along these lines, the positive racial appeals scores consider where candidates make campaign appearances. To measure these appearances, I used two cues from newspaper articles—the location of the candidate's appearance and the article's descriptors of the audience. Newspaper articles on candidates who campaign at race-neutral locations such as public parks, county fairs, factories, or schools with no descriptors of the racial composition of the audience are given a score of 0 on the positive racialization measure. The only exception regarding these venues was if the location is well known as having a large black population such as in South Central Los Angeles in

TABLE 1. Issues for racialized coding for articles

None = 0	Implicit = 1	Explicit = 2
Economy	Redistributive policies	Affirmative action
Tax cuts	Welfare	Civil rights legislation
Environment	Minimum wage	Busing
Campaign finance reform	Unemployment	Issues connected by candidate
Healthcare	Crime	to race
Infrastructure	Felon disenfranchisement	
Gay rights	Drugs	
Gambling	Capital punishment	
Education		
Military		
Non-African foreign affairs		
Energy policy		
Gun control		
Abortion		

1982, which would receive a score of 1. If the candidate speaks at a forum or gives an interview to an organization or media outlet known for its over- whelming black audience, the article is given a score of 2. For example, when it was reported that 2006 Tennessee U.S. Senate candidate Harold Ford Jr. visited Memphis to energize black voters, this article was given a 2 on the racialization scale. Moreover, if a candidate gave a speech at a black church, black college, or NAACP forum, then the article received a score of 2. For example, when 1989 Virginia gubernatorial candidate Douglas Wilder spoke at Virginia State University, a historically black college, he received a score of 2. Moreover, if a candidate gave an interview to media outlets such *Ebony* magazine or BET, whose audiences are predominantly African American, the article's positive racialization score would also be 2. Finally, if the crowd the candidate speaks to is described as majority black, then regardless of whether it is a race-neutral location, the candidate would receive a score of 2 on the positive racialization measure.

RACIALLY CODED LANGUAGE

Beyond the issues and the audience, the most direct determinant of whether a black candidate is appealing to the black community is what they say. Racially coded language, as defined by McIlwain and Caliendo (2011), utilizes the first or third person plural (us, we, they). Of course in campaign appearances, the audience matters. If a black Democrat speaks to a group of Democrats and uses the word *us*, the candidate is more likely referring to fellow Democrats. However, if a black candidate is speaking at a black church and uses the words *us* and *we*, this would be coded as a 2, an explicit appeal to the black community.

In coding the candidates' language, candidates who do not mention racial issues or do not use *us* or *they* language in racial contexts receive a score of 0. When candidates say they will represent "all" voters, for example, they are given a score of 0. Moreover, if the candidate says that race will not influence their decisions or will not hinder or advance their candidacy, they receive a score of 0. While these comments may draw attention to race, they do not demonstrate the candidate's intentions to advance the interests of the black electorate. If anything, they illustrate that racial considerations are not on the candidate's agenda.[55]

The candidates are also considered to make explicit appeals to black voters if they tie their biography to their race. For example, 1988 Virginia U.S. Senate candidate Maurice Dawkins mentioned in an interview that "he was the only black student at his Chicago high school."[56] Articles with this and similar statements are given the score of 2 because black candidates are showing that they are part of the black community. Finally, articles are given a score of 2 if the candidates have advertisements where either they or another African American uses *us* or *we* in reference to the candidate.

APPEARANCES WITH PROMINENT FIGURES

To appeal to a subset of voters, candidates will often appear or associate in gatherings with certain public officials. For instance, in his 2008 presidential campaign, Obama appeared with Massachusetts senators Ted Kennedy and John Kerry to help him win the state. Conversely, candidates who do not want to be associated with a politician or public figure will avoid being seen with them and downplay any relationships (past or present). For instance, during the 2008 campaign for the Democratic presidential nomination in which Hillary Clinton and Barack Obama squared off, Bill Clinton tried to tie Obama to Louis Farrakhan, the controversial Nation of Islam leader who endorsed Obama, but Obama distanced himself from Farrakhan by retorting, "I have been very clear in my denunciation of Farrakhan's history of anti-Semitic remarks, and I did not solicit his support."[57] Along these lines, black candidates Harvey Gantt (D-NC, 1990) and Tom Bradley (D-CA, 1982 and 1986) displayed their independence from the black community by reportedly asking Jesse Jackson and other black politicians to stay out of their campaigns.

In addition to the previous criteria, the articles are scored based on who the candidates campaigned with and who appears in their advertisements. If black candidates campaign with white public figures, they are given a score of 0. Candidates who campaign with black public figures who are not associated with a group that specifically advances black interests are given a score of 1. For example, when 2010 Florida U.S. Senate candidate Kendrick Meek campaigned with President Obama, he was scored as *implicitly* appealing to the black community. This was not considered an explicit appeal because Obama does not assert a progressive black agenda. The same is true if a candidate campaigns with black celebrities such as actor James Earl Jones, as Carol Moseley Braun did in 1992 when she successfully ran for U.S. Senate in Illinois. Articles are given a score of 2 if the candidates campaigned with or touted the endorsement of a black public figure who champions black political interests or has been tied to an organization that advances black interests. For example, candidates who campaign with Jesse Jackson, who has been a strong and vocal civil rights proponent, are given a score of 2. A candidate who publicizes his or her ties to such public figures sends the message that he or she will advance the black community's interests. Such an association makes an explicit appeal to the black community.

Negative Racial Appeals

In addition to measuring positive racial appeals, candidates are also scored on their negative racial appeals. Most often these come in the form of verbal attacks on an opponent, party, or supposed political ally. Thus, unlike positive racial appeals, they were not measured on multiple dimensions (audience, associations, and issues). Moreover, given that all negative racial appeals are explicit, they can be coded dichotomously. If the candidate did not attack his or her opponent, did not mention race, or discusses race in a positive way, the article received a score of 0 on this negative racialization measure. If the black candidate accused his or her opponent of playing the race card or injecting race into the campaign, they received a score of 1. For example, when Deval Patrick's 2006 campaign manager argued that their opponent, Republican Kerry Healey, was playing the race card in several advertisements, the Patrick campaign was given a score of 1 on this measure.

While it is only fair for candidates who face discrimination in a campaign to identify these attacks as racist, in doing so they run the risk of appearing as overly sensitive. In response to a Republican National Committee commercial that was widely reported as playing on racial stereotypes, black candidate Harold Ford Jr. (D-TN, 2006) argued that the advertisement had nothing to do with race but instead was in poor taste.[58] Later in his book *More*

Davids than Goliaths, Ford said that while he thought the ad did use racially coded appeals, he feared that any mention of race or racism would lead to a backlash against his campaign. "I was not going to go on TV and call the ad racist. That was what the Corker's campaign wanted me to do. It would be the lead story on every network, and it risked alienating voters."[59] Moreover, by making these accusations, the candidate risks calling attention to race without discussing ways to address black political interests. While other news organizations identified the RNC advertisement as being racially divisive, Ford and his campaign remained above the fray.

Candidates who argue that racism is limiting their opportunities as reported in an article are also given a score of 1 for the negative racialization measure. For example, 2008 Mississippi U.S. Senate candidate Erik Fleming accused the Democratic Senatorial Campaign Committee of withholding financial support from himself and fellow Democrat Vivian Davis Figures in Alabama because they were black candidates running in southern states.[60] Similar claims were made by Alan Keyes against the Republican Party in his 1992 campaign for the U.S. Senate in Maryland. In such cases, the candidates argue that racism within their party or other organizations is limiting their electoral opportunities. As a result, they are making a negative racial appeal.

Moreover, black candidates who make race-based attacks on others are also given a score of 1 on the negative racialization measure. The 1990 South Carolina gubernatorial candidate Theo Mitchell was given a score of 1 on this measure because he complained about black leaders who did not support him. "These are the individuals we must expose. And let it be known that black leadership is no longer going to be this type to sell out its people. These are Uncle Toms."[61] Along the same lines, 1988 Virginia U.S. Senate candidate Maurice Dawkins received a score of 1 on the negative racialization scale when a newspaper reported that he had accused his opponent as having a "plantation mentality" because of his poor treatment of blacks.[62] While these claims may attract some black support, they also highlight race in a divisive manner and do little to demonstrate the candidate's intentions of overcoming racial barriers.

Candidates can simultaneously make positive and negative racial appeals. For example, while Theo Mitchell chastised black public figures for not supporting him, he also mentioned that his candidacy would "speak out against this for young black youths who are looking to us for leadership. We must denounce our own who are betraying us."[63] In this scenario, the article received a score of 1 for negative racial appeals given that he explicitly attacked black public figures based on race for endorsing his opponent. It was also given a score of 2 for positive racial appeals because Mitchell explicitly outlined his goal of protecting the black youth.

Chapter Outline and Summaries

The book is divided into two sections. The first examines black candidates who campaigned for the U.S. Senate or governor between 1982 and 2010 and voters' reactions to their campaigns. Chapter 1 provides an overview of the diversity of black candidates who campaign for high-profile statewide office through the disaggregation of these candidates into five classifications: Nonracialized Rule Follower, Racialized Rule Follower, Right Candidate at the Wrong Time, Racialized Longshot, and Go Quietly. These classifications demonstrate the vast differences in levels of viability among these candidates and the variety of racial campaign tactics that they use. Moreover, the five classifications highlight that both successful and unsuccessful black candidates run deracialized campaigns, and this raises questions about the efficacy of a deracialized campaign strategy. While I do not use these categories in the empirical analysis, this categorization exercise provides information about the types of black candidates who campaign for high-profile elected office in majority white settings.

Chapter 2 examines whether black candidates' use of racial appeals influences black, white, and/or Latino voter turnout using the racialization measures outlined in this chapter and the Current Population Survey's Voter Supplement from 1982 to 2010. While a number of studies suggest that black candidates who run deracialized campaigns have a difficult time mobilizing black voters, the results presented in chapter 2 indicate that racial appeals do not significantly affect voter turnout when controlling for other factors such as the candidate's political affiliation, political experience, and the region in which they campaign. However, positive racial appeals increase Latino turnout by statistically significant and substantial margins.

Following this analysis, chapter 3 uses state exit poll data for twenty-seven elections to explore whether black candidates who use racial appeals garner more black, white, and/or Latino votes. The results of chapter 3 demonstrate that positive racial appeals increase black support for black candidates without diminishing support from white or Latino voters. In fact, the results of chapter 3 indicate that Latino voters are much more supportive of black candidates who make positive racial appeals. Conversely, black candidates who utilize negative racial appeals perform worse among black and white voters. Overall, this chapter finds that black candidates can make race-based appeals and still succeed in electoral politics. However, their success is contingent on whether they racialize in a negative or positive manner.

The second section further investigates the relationship between racialization and political behavior by moving beyond the state level. Chapters 4,

5, and 6 compare voters' reactions to the campaign style of Jesse Jackson in his 1984 and 1988 White House bids and Barack Obama's in 2008. The comparison provides more leverage to the study by demonstrating that similar electoral responses to the use of racialization at the state level also occur at the national level with much more high-profile black candidates. Moreover, the examination of these campaigns allows us to better understand the temporal ordering of racial appeals and changes in electoral support and the mechanisms that influence the efficacy of race-based appeals.

In chapter 4, I use state primary exit polls from 1988 and 2008 and the American National Election Studies from 1988 and 2008 to determine whether Barack Obama or Jesse Jackson increased voter turnout or received more votes from black, white, and Latino voters in the Democratic primary.[64] While I do not find significant differences in black turnout in either election, I do find that black voters prefer racialized black candidates, such as Jackson, over their post-racial counterparts. I find that Obama, the deracialized black candidate, performed better among Latino and white voters. I discuss how differences in Jackson's campaign compared with those of the average black U.S. Senate or gubernatorial candidate may explain these contradictory findings.

To examine the temporal ordering of racial appeals and changes in electoral support among various racial/ethnic groups, chapter 5 investigates whether voter support for Obama and Jackson changes after high-profile positive and negative racial appeals. For the former, I analyze voters' reactions to Obama's major race speech during the 2008 Democratic presidential primary entitled "A More Perfect Union." For the latter, I assess how voters respond to Jesse Jackson's anti-Semitic remarks in the 1984 presidential election. The remarks themselves do not represent a negative racial appeal. However, Jackson's response to the criticism about the remarks suggested that he was being persecuted because of his race. In combination, an examination of voters' responses to these two high-profile racial appeals allows us to assess the temporal ordering of racialization and levels of voter support for black candidates. The results of this chapter provide more evidence to support the results presented in chapters 3 and 4. Following the More Perfect Union speech, Obama performed better among both blacks and Latinos and did not sacrifice support from white voters. Conversely, following the "Hymietown" controversy in Jackson's 1984 presidential campaign, Jackson experienced a significant decrease in support among voters of all races.

Chapter 6 explores *why* black voters prefer black candidates who use positive racial appeals. To accomplish this goal, I return to the candidacies of Obama and Jackson and the 1988 and 2008 American National Election

Studies. The findings reveal that blacks feel that racialized black candidates *care* about them. This perception of empathy more than likely explains why black voters are more supportive of black candidates who appeal to the African American community in a positive manner.

In the concluding chapter, I discuss the implications of my findings for African Americans and their politics. While successful bids by black candidates in high-profile races depend on many more factors than a racial strategy, I argue that black voters are rational and do not automatically support black candidates who fail to appeal to their community. I discuss how the results inform us about how black candidates should address race in their campaigns to maximize their success in majority white settings. I conclude this chapter with a normative discussion of what the racial moderation of black politicians may mean for black political and economic progress and how a reversal of these trends may improve conditions in the black community.

1

What Are My Choices?

THE GROWING DIVERSITY IN HIGH-PROFILE
STATEWIDE BLACK CANDIDATES

In 2004, two major party African American candidates competed for Illinois's U.S. Senate seat. The Democratic nominee was Barack Obama, who ran a campaign that was celebrated for its ability to reach across the aisle. In endorsing Obama, the Springfield *State-Journal Register* noted that "Obama receives our support for many reasons, but one of the most striking differences between these candidates comes down to inclusiveness versus exclusiveness. Obama represents the former."[1] One viewer of the 2004 Democratic National Convention praised Obama for his centrist appeal. "I watched a little of the convention . . . and was unimpressed with most of the Bush bashing. However, that Barack Obama is one to watch. He is very charismatic and stayed away from most of the partisan rhetoric. If he manages to keep a centrist message, he may well be our first black president."[2] In addition to Obama's skilled and well organized campaign, he was fortunate to be the Democratic nominee in a left-leaning state that had previously elected a black U.S. senator.

Even more fortuitous for Obama was that his black Republican opponent, Alan Keyes, ran a campaign that alienated even the most conservative voters. Keyes hoped to gain traction by making inflammatory statements, and as one *Chicago Tribune* writer noted, he did not disappoint.[3] During the course of the campaign, Keyes equated abortion with terrorism.[4] He later argued that Jesus would not vote for Obama because of his support for pro-choice policies.[5] Keyes's problems with voters went beyond his controversial campaign style. Keyes was not from Illinois and was too conservative for many voters in the state. The only reason he was on the ballot was because the previous Republican nominee, Jack Ryan, had resigned after a scandal involving his ex-wife. The poor timing of Keyes's candidacy and his undisciplined campaign strategy helped Obama win the U.S. Senate seat by almost a three-to-one margin.

The 2004 Illinois U.S. Senate election provides both a perfect example of how black candidates should campaign if they hope to succeed in majority white contexts and a good example of how black candidates can sabotage their candidacies. Several political scientists suggest that for black candidates to prosper they must campaign on issues that transcend race. They must also have significant political experience and campaign in a favorable political context.[6] Obama satisfied all of these criteria, whereas Keyes did not. The differences in these two campaigns are emblematic of the wide range of black candidates who compete for high-profile statewide office. Some candidates have significant political experience and run in favorable settings, but focus on racial issues. Others have significant political experience, and they run deracialized campaigns, but compete against well-qualified opponents in politically unfriendly contexts. Still others, like Alan Keyes, follow none of the prescribed criteria.

The growing number of high-profile statewide black candidates has yielded a lot of diversity in these candidates' qualifications, campaign strategies, and partisanship. Additionally, they are campaigning in vastly different contexts, and the quality of their opponents varies significantly. Using this diversity, I disaggregate U.S. Senate and gubernatorial black candidates into five categories: Nonracialized Rule Follower, Racialized Rule Follower, Right Candidate at the Wrong Time, Racialized Longshot, and Go Quietly.[7] These categories are created using prescribed criteria that black candidates should follow if they hope to succeed in majority white contexts. In particular, the candidates will be disaggregated based on whether they ran a racialized campaign, as measured by the criteria outlined in the first chapter, their levels of political experience, and the political context in which they campaign. The review of these candidates will provide a contextual understanding for the campaigns I analyze in the first half of this study.

How Black Candidates Can Succeed in Majority White Settings

In spite of the precipitous growth in the number of black candidates campaigning for high-profile statewide office, the fact remains that few will succeed in their quest to be governor or U.S. senator. One of the primary reasons for their dismal success rate is that blacks form no more than 40 percent of the population in any state and no more than 21 percent of the population in states outside of the South.[8] Thus black candidates must rely on a large number of often reluctant racial crossover voters in order to succeed.[9] While there may be some disagreement about what it takes for black candidates to prosper in these majority white contexts, many social scientists and accomplished black politicians agree that most competitive black candidates will have similar characteristics.

Political scientists and pundits argue that black candidates should de-emphasize race and steer clear of racially divisive issues and political figures to increase their appeal to white voters, who make up the plurality or majority of voters in every state.[10] By focusing on issues that transcend race and

TABLE 2. Candidate types and characteristics

Candidate type	Deracialized campaign	Significant political experience	Favorable electoral conditions
Nonracialized Rule Follower	X	X	X
Racialized Rule Follower	–	X	/
Right Candidate, Wrong Time	X	X	–
Racialized Longshot	–	–	–
Go Quietly	X	–	–

X = Indicates that the candidates satisfied this criterion.
/ = Indicates that the candidates partially satisfied this criterion.
– = Indicates that the candidates did not satisfy this criterion.

demonstrating their political independence from the black community, black candidates can minimize concerns that they will favor one racial/ethnic group.

Some have suggested that black candidates have a more difficult time appearing viable without previous elected experience. Senator Edward W. Brooke III (R-MA. 1966–78), the first African American elected to the U.S. Senate since Reconstruction, noted, "It is not only important for the black candidate to be as qualified as his white counterpart, . . . in most cases you have to be twice as good as your white competitor if you hope to stand a chance."[11] A substantial percentage of white voters believe that all else being equal, white candidates are better suited for elected office than their black counterparts.[12] To offset this stereotype, black candidates should have significant political credentials.

Others contend that blacks have the best opportunities to succeed in states that favor their political party.[13] Given that black candidates face a number of disadvantages, including lower levels of support from white voters and difficulties raising funds, they are most likely to overcome these disadvantages if they campaign in friendly political contexts. Some have suggested that Obama's victory in 2008 was substantially bolstered by the Democratic-friendly political climate.[14] Table 2 summarizes these attributes and displays the different categories of black candidates and which criteria they satisfied. Table 3 lists the candidates in each category.

Nonracialized Rule Follower

Every once in a while, everything falls into place. The Nonracialized Rule Followers satisfy all of the prescribed guidelines that are necessary for them to succeed in majority white electorates. As a result, four of the seven black candidates in this category have been successful in their bids for statewide office, and the three who failed lost in very close elections. Most of the candidates in this category have significant political experience. Some, such as 1982 California gubernatorial candidate Tom Bradley and 1990 North Carolina U.S. Senate candidate Harvey Gantt, served as mayors of large cities. In addition to their experience, these candidates de-emphasize race in their campaigns. The 1992 Illinois U.S. Senate candidate Carol Moseley Braun, for example, ran on a platform that emphasized women's rights and lowering taxes for the middle class. Tom Bradley's campaign focused on controlling crime by advocating for harsher penalties for criminals. Moreover, many of these candidates demonstrated their independence from the black community by avoiding other black leaders and appearances before majority black audiences. *Washington Post* reporter Huntington Williams notes that 1990 U.S. Senate candidate Gantt, unlike his white predecessor, 1984 Democratic U.S. Senate nominee Jim Hunt, stayed away from other African American political figures. "Unlike Hunt's campaign in 1984, when Jesse L. Jackson made much-publicized voter registration visits to North Carolina . . . Gantt's effort was very low-profile. Jackson and other black politicians have reportedly been asked to stay out of North Carolina for this race."[15] While many political commentators praised these candidates for their post-racial campaigns, several faced criticism from the black community for not doing enough to represent their interests.[16] These candidates coincidently did not vary in their partisanship. All of the Nonracialized Rule Followers represented the Democratic Party.

Their abilities and experience are not the only things going in their favor. The Nonracialized Rule Followers also campaign in states that hold favorable views of their parties. Deval Patrick, Obama, and Moseley Braun ran in Massachusetts and Illinois, which have a long history of supporting Democrats and black politicians. Only one of these candidates ran against an incumbent, and most had more political experience than their opponent. Deval Patrick's 2010 campaign for governor of Massachusetts exemplifies the candidates in this category.

Deval Patrick

In 2010, Deval Patrick became the first African American to run for reelection as governor. Despite being the incumbent, and thus more experienced for the position than his opponents, the economic recession in Massachusetts made Patrick's reelection bid far from certain. Several polls conducted by the *Boston Globe* early in 2010 showed that a majority of the electorate was unhappy with Patrick's performance.[17] To make matters worse, Patrick was a

TABLE 3. Candidates by type

Nonracialized Rule Follower	Racialized Rule Follower	Right Candidate, Wrong Time	Racialized Longshot	Go Quietly
Tom Bradley (1982 CA)	Douglas Wilder (1989 VA)	Tom Bradley (1986 CA)	William Lucas (1986 MI)	Jack Robinson (2000 MA)
Harvey Gantt (1990 NC)	Harvey Gantt (1996 NC)	Ron Sims (1994 WA)	Maurice Dawkins (1988 VA)	Troy Brown (2000 MS)
Carol Moseley Braun (1992 IL)	Carl McCall (2002 NY)	Alan Wheat (1994 MO)	Alan Keyes (1988 MD)	Joseph Neal (2002 NV)
Carol Moseley Braun (1998 IL)	Ron Kirk (2002 TX)	Gary Franks (1998 CT)	Theo Mitchell (1990 SC)	Marvin Scott (2004 IN)
Barack Obama (2004 IL)	Michael Steele (2006 MD)	Denise Majette (2004 GA)	Alan Keyes (1992 MD)	Wayne Sowell (2004 AL)
Deval Patrick (2006 MA)	Harold Ford Jr. (2006 TN)	Kenneth Blackwell (2006 OH)	Cleo Fields (1995 LA)	Erik Fleming (2008 MS)
Deval Patrick (2010 MA)		Lynn Swann (2006 PA)	Alan Keyes (2004 IL)	Vivian Figures (2008 Al)
		Michael Thurmond (2010 GA)	Erik Fleming (2006 MS)	Alvin Greene (2010 SC)
		Kendrick Meek (2010 FL)		

Democrat in a year when Democrats were unpopular. Even the consistently Democratic state of Massachusetts had elected a Republican, Scott Brown, to the U.S. Senate earlier in the year.

While the context in some ways was hostile for Patrick, several things went in his favor. First, he ran unchallenged in the primaries and had the strong support of his party. Second, he would benefit from the independent candidacy of Tim Cahill, who previously served as state treasurer. Cahill was very well funded, and his campaign siphoned off many key votes from the Republican nominee, Charlie Baker. The inclusion of two candidates split the Republican vote and gave Patrick the opportunity to be reelected in a tough economic climate. Finally, Democrats maintained a three-to-one registration advantage over Republicans in Massachusetts.[18] Even in an unfavorable year for Democrats, Patrick still ran in a state that overwhelmingly supported his party.

Like the other candidates in this category, Deval Patrick's reelection campaign focused on issues that transcend race. In particular, he focused mostly on economic issues. While the unemployment rate and the deficit grew in Massachusetts during Patrick's tenure, he explained that the measures he took as governor, including raising the sales tax, helped prevent

Massachusetts from declining as much as other big states such as California. He also highlighted his opponents' mismanagement of the construction project known as the "Big Dig" to illustrate that they did not have the capability to bring Massachusetts out of the recession.[19] Patrick's opponents also shied away from racial issues. Instead, his opponents primarily attacked Patrick on fiscal issues. They also argued that Massachusetts would be better served with a divided government.

As the campaign progressed, many of Cahill's supporters began to switch their allegiance to Republican Charlie Baker. Despite large defections of Cahill supporters, Deval Patrick was able to win reelection with less than a majority (48 percent). Overall, his qualifications as someone who could succeed at the state level, his centrist nonracialized campaign strategy, Massachusetts's left-leaning electorate, and the good fortune of having two conservative leaning candidates in the election helped Patrick become the first African American to be reelected as governor.

Racialized Rule Follower

Generally, black candidates with significant political experience do not use racial appeals in their campaigns. However, there are instances in which viable black candidates utilize subtle or even overt appeals to members of their racial group to mobilize their base. The Racialized Rule Followers all have significant political experience. Some, like 2006 Maryland U.S. Senate candidate Michael Steele and 2002 New York gubernatorial candidate Carl McCall, held state offices. Others, like 2006 Tennessee U.S. Senate candidate Harold Ford Jr., were prominent congressional representatives. While these candidates do not always campaign in the most supportive political contexts, almost all in this category ran for an open seat rather than campaigning against an entrenched incumbent. Moreover, many of these candidates took centrist positions. Ford ran a campaign in which he highlighted his religion and advocated for fewer regulations for gun owners. Michael Steele supported more stringent limits on stem cell research and advocated for a federal ban on gay marriages.

While the Racialized Rule Followers share many of the same attributes as their nonracialized counterparts, they do not completely ignore race. In fact, many use what Franklin (2010) describes as a situational deracialization strategy. According to Franklin, these candidates present a deracialized portrait of themselves to majority white audiences and many media outlets. As a result, they advocate for the same issues as their nonracialized counterparts. However, candidates who use a situational deracialization strategy also use positive race-conscious appeals to black audiences and make a concerted effort to demonstrate their symbolic connection to the black community. Thus it is not uncommon for Racialized Rule Followers to highlight the positive implications of their candidacies for the black community. Ford, for example, made several racial appeals including telling a black church, "If you fight for me for the next forty-eight hours against these forces that want to turn us back, I will fight for you every single day in the United States Senate."[20] In an attempt to mobilize the black youth, Michael Steele posted on his Facebook page that he "was hip-hoppin' his way into the U.S. Senate," and he enlisted several black celebrities including Don King, Russell Simmons, and Mike Tyson to campaign on his behalf.[21] While an examination of only issue preferences may lead one to conclude that these candidates used a deracialized strategy, a broader definition of racialization would reveal that these candidates did attempt to appeal to black voters though the use of positive race-conscious appeals. The 2002 Texas U.S. Senate nominee Ron Kirk provides a good example of a candidate in this category.

Ron Kirk

In 1994, Ron Kirk became the first African American to be elected mayor of Dallas. Given strong support from former governor Ann Richards and high levels of turnout from the black community, Kirk was elected in a city in which black voters barely account for a quarter of the population. Kirk's high approval ratings allowed him to be reelected in 1998. In 2002, Kirk left the mayor's office to pursue a U.S. Senate seat vacated by Phil Gramm. Kirk was the favorite of several high-profile Democrats in the primaries and handily defeated his opponent Victor Morales. Ron Kirk's nomination excited Democrats who believed that his experience and high approval ratings in one of Texas's largest cities made him a formidable candidate to compete for the open U.S. Senate seat. Moreover, Kirk's nomination coincided with Democrats nominating a Latino gubernatorial candidate and a white lieutenant gubernatorial candidate. The diversity of the candidates at the top of the Democrats' state ticket was dubbed the "Dream Team."[22]

While Kirk certainly held some liberal positions, including his initial lack of support for a proposed war in Iraq, supporting bans on drilling in Alaska, and increasing funding for education in poorer communities, he also held a number of conservative positions. Following the September 11, 2001, attacks, Ron Kirk was a strong proponent of increasing spending for the Department of Homeland Security and the defense budget. He supported the Bush tax cuts and was in favor of extending them in the future. He also appealed to conservatives and moderates in the state by advocating for fewer restrictions on gun ownership. In addition to running a centrist campaign, Kirk was able to deal a blow to John Cornyn's candidacy by tying him to the failed energy giant Enron, which had recently been charged with insider trading and artificially manipulating the energy market. All of these factors made Kirk a credible and competitive candidate in conservative Texas.

While Ron Kirk took several moderate-to-conservative policy stances, he made several positive racial appeals to the black community. First, Kirk was a proponent of affirmative action and any policy that could lead to more equitable outcomes for minority students.[23] Second, Kirk argued that he would be careful about supporting the war in Iraq because minorities would be disproportionately affected by the decision to go to war.[24] Finally, Kirk appeared with several rap artists in an event to mobilize young black voters. The event garnered a lot of media attention and was used by his Republican opponent, John Cornyn, to argue that Kirk was trying to inject race into the campaign.

Ron Kirk's centrist positions and his ability to mobilize black voters kept him within ten points of his opponent in most pre-election polls. However, in a year in which homeland security was important, Kirk's wavering support for the Iraq war was particularly damaging. In the end, he was defeated. In spite of his double-digit defeat, Kirk ran a very competitive campaign, and his positive racial appeals appeared to inspire blacks. Rapper Tracy Curry said this about Kirk's campaign: "This is a funny thing coming from me because it's my first time voting, Ron Kirk as a brother in the Senate? Come on, man. It's clear what that means."[25]

Right Candidate at the Wrong Time

The candidates in the Right Candidate at the Wrong Time category run predominately deracialized campaigns and have significant political experience. These candidates also appeal to the median voter by running as centrists, and most enjoy the strong support of their party. However, most are political underdogs because of outside circumstances. Many of these candidates run against popular incumbents. For example, California gubernatorial candidate Tom Bradley in 1986 ran against an incumbent who had a 73 percent approval rating a year before the election.[26] Others run in states that have a history of supporting the black candidate's opposing party. Denise Majette was the 2004 Democratic U.S. Senate nominee in the state of Georgia, which had supported the Republican presidential nominee in all but one election since 1980.

Other candidates in this category are nominees in political climates that are hostile to their political party. Democratic U.S. Senate nominees Ron Sims (D-WA) and Alan Wheat (D-MO) ran in 1994 when the Democratic Party lost a large number of seats in the House of Representatives. Ken Blackwell (D-OH) ran as a Republican in 2006 when voters were pushing back against the agenda of Republican president George W. Bush. The conditions surrounding these candidates' campaigns usually leads them to lose by large margins (generally greater than 20 percent) despite their best efforts. In sum, many lack what Jones and Clemons (1993) describe as the luck or "wild card" that many black candidates needed to succeed in majority white settings. Tom Bradley's 1986 bid to be governor of California is in many ways representative of the Right Candidate at the Wrong Time category.

Tom Bradley

In 1982, many believed that Los Angeles mayor Tom Bradley would become the first black governor in U.S. history. Bradley led by a significant margin in pre-election polls leading up to the 1982 election, but was defeated by less than 2 percent. Four years after his close defeat, Bradley ran again and easily won the Democratic primary with more than 80 percent of the vote.

Bradley ran a deracialized campaign in the general election in the same style that had brought him so close to victory four years earlier. When questioned by reporters about race, Bradley consistently responded that race would not play a role in his election or defeat.[27] He also touted his ability to win reelection twice in Los Angeles, a city where 20 percent of residents are black. When Jesse Jackson endorsed Bradley two years after his controversial 1984 bid for president, Bradley distanced himself from Jackson rather than embracing his endorsement. This decision angered some black supporters who were already wary of Bradley's interest in advocating for the black community.[28]

Bradley also campaigned on issues that are most often associated with the Republican Party. In particular, Bradley ran on a law and order platform. Bradley introduced a nine-point drug plan that included harsher sentences for drug dealers.[29] He also supported the death penalty, a position that would put him at odds with some Democratic voters. Bradley pointed to his record as a police officer and touted his support from the police unions in Los Angeles as evidence that he would be the governor who was most concerned with crime.

Unfortunately, the conditions that made Bradley competitive in 1982 were absent in 1986. In particular, Bradley was not campaigning for an open seat, but instead was challenging a popular incumbent governor. During his first term in office, Bradley's Republican opponent, George Deukmejian, consistently had approval ratings of over 70 percent. Bradley was also no longer the frontrunner and was not as qualified as his opponent, who had already served a full term as governor of the nation's most populated state. Rising crime rates in Los Angeles during this period also made it easier for

Deukmejian to exploit stereotypes that blacks were weak on crime. Despite running a campaign that should have appealed to many independent voters and to the then majority white population, Bradley was soundly defeated by more than 20 percent in 1986. He received 12 percent less support from the electorate in 1986 than he did in 1982, despite running a very similar campaign, enjoying comparable levels of black turnout, and raising a similar amount of money.

Racialized Longshot

The Racialized Longshot candidates are often characterized by their explicit appeals to the black community and their low probability of success. It is not uncommon for these candidates to focus almost exclusively on race when they campaign for governor or senator. However, unlike the Racialized Rule Followers, these candidates use both positive and negative racial appeals. Along these lines, these candidates often attack their opponents for not doing enough for the black community, without offering proposals for how they would govern differently.

In addition to their often divisive racial appeals, there are many other factors that make it difficult for these black candidates to succeed. They campaign in a state where their partisanship is out of step with the average voter, they most often run against popular incumbents, and they lack significant political experience. Racialized Longshots often win their primaries because of lack of interest from other politicians who are concerned about their ability to succeed in an unfavorable context. For example, rather than win a competitive primary, Alan Keyes was drafted by the Republican Party twice (1988-MD, 2004-IL) to run against a popular Democratic candidate. Theo Mitchell provides a good example of a Racialized Longshot candidate.

Theo Mitchell

In 1990, Republican South Carolina governor Carroll Campbell Jr. was considered unbeatable. A couple of years earlier, the state had completed its transformation from being reliably Democratic to staunchly Republican. Moreover, a vast majority of potential voters in South Carolina had favorable ratings of the incumbent. Campbell's approval ratings weren't just confined to the state's large number of Republican voters; even large segments of the Democratic Party backed his candidacy. Campbell's popularity scared off many otherwise viable Democratic candidates. In the Democratic primary, only two candidates with any experience competed for the nomination, and both were state senators. Mitchell benefited from the state's large black population. This in combination with white Democrats' apathy about the white nominee, given Campbell's popularity, helped Mitchell win the nomination.

For most of the campaign cycle, Mitchell focused on improving education funding and closing tax loopholes for corporate interests. Despite his attention to these and other nonracial issues, Mitchell was hurt by comments he made early in the campaign cycle about black public figures who endorsed his white opponent over him. In response to a black mayor endorsing Campbell, Mitchell complained, "I think he's another one of the black prostitutes who have sold out their race, their dignity, their honor, and their integrity, just like those three or four black mayors did at Port Royal. It is a disgrace to see that he is still a slave in the last part of the twentieth century."[30] Mitchell also made a number of race-based attacks on his opponent. In one instance, Mitchell argued that comments Campbell made during the 1970s incited a race riot that led to the injuries of several black children.[31] Comments like these quickly made race a salient issue in the campaign, but did so in a way that many people saw as divisive.

While Mitchell was unlikely to succeed regardless of his message, his racial language further weakened his candidacy. Not only did very few white voters support Mitchell's candidacy but a sizable portion of the black community also supported his opponent. In one pre-election poll, Mitchell only received the support of 61 percent of black voters in South Carolina.[32] In the end, he received less than 30 percent of the vote in the general election in a state where blacks make up a third of the population.

Go Quietly

While the Racialized Longshot candidates attract substantial media attention because of their controversial candidacies, the Go Quietlies generally receive less coverage. Like the Racialized Longshot candidates, Go Quietlies generally have little or no elected experience. Some, such as 2000 Massachusetts U.S. Senate candidate Jack E. Robinson and 2004 Indiana U.S. Senate candidate Marvin Scott, worked in the private sector, and others, such as 2010 South Carolina U.S. Senate candidate Alvin Greene, were unemployed when campaigning for elected office. All of these candidates challenge popular incumbents, and most do not face serious opposition in the primary. For example, 2002 Nevada gubernatorial candidate Joseph Neal's two largest competitors in the Democratic primary were a reformed stripper and the option "none of these candidates." To make matters worse, these candidates run in states that traditionally do not support their party. More often than not, they are Democrats who are running in the Deep South. Democrats Erik

Fleming (D-MS, 2006, 2008), Troy Brown (D-MS, 2000), Wayne Sowell (D-AL, 2004), Vivian Figures (D-AL, 2008), and Alvin Greene (D-SC, 2010) all ran in southern Republican strongholds. Given these candidates' lack of experience and poor prospects for electoral success, they often receive less coverage than other black candidates. While Joseph Neal of Nevada received more coverage than other black candidates in this category, his candidacy is representative of the Go Quietlies.

Joseph Neal

Black candidate Joe Neal was a Nevada state senator before he decided to run for governor in 2002. Republican governor Kenny Guinn had high approval ratings, and the Democratic Party was expected to perform poorly in a year when voters were concerned with national security, an issue that usually favors the Republican Party. As a result, the 2002 Democratic gubernatorial primary held few viable contenders. In fact, Neal's biggest competitor in the primaries was the "none of these candidates" option, which he only defeated by 10 percent of the vote. When asked about the primary, Neal said, "It's just an embarrassing thing for candidates like me when you're trying to make a difference, and you have to look back and see if 'none' is going to beat you."[33]

Joe Neal's lackluster support in the primaries carried over into the general election. Despite running as a major party candidate, Neal received little financial support from the Democratic Party and the public. He only raised $50,000 to compete against Kenny Guinn's $3 million. Guinn had such a large fund-raising advantage that during the middle of the election cycle Guinn turned down donations, saying that he was not going to need it.[34] Neal's lack of fund-raising made it impossible to hire a professional staff or advertise his candidacy. Moreover, given Guinn's large lead, there was no televised debate. While Neal championed issues that would appeal to Democratic voters, such as universal health care, increased spending for education, and creation of a more equitable tax system, his lack of financial support and media coverage made it difficult to disseminate his platform to potential supporters. As a result, most voters knew very little about Neal's campaign. Some newspapers noted that a large segment of the Nevada electorate did not even know that Kenny Guinn was being challenged.[35]

As the campaign progressed, it became evident that Neal was not going to defeat Guinn. The election was so uncompetitive that Guinn left the campaign trail and began to plan his second term. Neal's inability to gain support throughout the campaign led him to stop focusing on even winning the election. Instead, he mentioned that his campaign was focusing more on combating the powerful gambling lobby in the state. Toward the end of the campaign Neal admitted, "I'm not running against Kenny Guinn. I'm running against gaming."[36] Neal also said the only reason he ran was to preserve a two-party system in Nevada.[37] Joe Neal's lackluster campaign was evident in the final result in which Kenny Guinn defeated him by a three-to-one margin.

Conclusion

More than forty-five years after the signing of the 1965 Voting Rights Act, there has been a large growth in the number of black candidates running for the most prestigious offices in the United States. This growth yields a dramatic increase in the diversity of these candidates' qualifications and produces a variety of campaign styles. Moreover, these high-profile black candidates campaign in various contexts and face opponents who range from long-term popular incumbents to political neophytes. Some high-profile black candidates are successful, others lose in competitive races, and a growing number of these candidates' campaigns fail to gain any traction. Most important for this project, these candidates differ in how they address race in their campaigns.

The review of these candidates demonstrates that racialized appeals are not specific to one type of black candidate. Black candidates with a wide range of competitiveness, from different political parties and in different regions of the country, vary in how they utilize racial appeals. For example, both Racialized Rule Followers and Nonracialized Rule Followers are competitive and have significant political experience. However, the Racialized Rule Followers are much more likely to make positive race-based appeals than their nonracialized counterparts. Moreover, some Republican candidates like Michael Steele and Alan Keyes use racial appeals, while others, such as Lynn Swann (R-PA, 2006) and Ken Blackwell (R-OH, 2006), de-emphasize their connections to black voters.

Not only is there variation in who racializes; there are also big differences in how candidates racialize. Racialized Rule Followers inject race into the campaign by highlighting their connections to the black community and advancing the policy concerns of black voters. Others, such as the Racialized Longshots, have taken a more racially divisive approach in which they use race to attack other political players. Ron Kirk, for example, was much more likely to discuss the positive implications of his campaign for black voters, whereas Theo Mitchell injected race into the campaign through attacks on his political opponents.

Given that both competitive and uncompetitive candidates utilize racial appeals, and successful and unsuccessful politicians run deracialized campaigns, the puzzle of the efficacy of race-based appeals remains. If the message of the black candidate is irrelevant, we should find that variation in their racial campaign strategy will have an inconsequential effect on black electoral support and turnout. Moreover, white and Latino voters should be as supportive of the Racialized Rule Followers as they are of their nonracialized counterparts. But if the racial message matters, we should find differences in electoral support for racialized and deracialized black candidates. Moreover, if the tone of the appeals influences political behavior differently, we should observe variation in electoral support even among racialized candidates when other factors are held constant. In the following chapters, I examine the influence that positive and negative racial appeals have on vote choice and turnout in more detail using statistical analysis of exit poll data and surveys collected by the U.S. Census. By accounting for a number of potentially confounding factors, I provide a better understanding of whether black candidates' electoral success can be attributed to how they address race in their campaigns.

2

Black Candidates and Voter Turnout

DOES RACIALIZATION MATTER?

Political pundits, candidates, and casual political observers often argue that the presence of a black candidate increases black voter turnout. Even President Barack Obama voiced this belief as he declared in 2007: "I guarantee you, African American turnout, if I'm the nominee, goes up 30 percent around the country, minimum."[1] Likewise *New York Times* contributor Gerald Benjamin stated in 2002, "If Carl McCall wins in the primary he will be the first major-party African-American nominee for governor of New York, offering New Yorkers a chance to make history. For that reason alone, his nomination is likely to increase turnout among black voters."[2] While scholars have found that black turnout does indeed increase when a black candidate is on the ballot,[3] most researchers who explore this voter turnout/black candidate relationship implicitly assume that African American voters respond to the campaigns of *all* black candidates equally.

Of studies examining the link between black candidates and turnout, only Ebonya Washington (2006) and Griffin and Keane (2006) take into account the differences in partisanship between candidates. Based on a comprehensive literature review, no studies examine whether black candidates' racial campaign styles—in terms of identifying with and voicing support for the black community or remaining race-neutral and distant from the black community—play a mediating role between their presence on the ballot and the mobilization of black voters beyond case studies of one or two black candidates. It is not yet known whether black candidates who use positive and/ or negative racial appeals in their campaigns, like Ron Kirk (D-TX, 2002) and Theo Mitchell (D-SC, 1990), respectively, inspire higher levels of black voter turnout than their counterparts who minimize the discussion of race in their bids for elected office such as Deval Patrick (D-MA, 2006, 2010) and Barack Obama.

This chapter examines whether black candidates' use of positive and/or negative racial appeals influences turnout. To accomplish this goal, I outline why an election's racial context may enhance or diminish black voter turnout.

I then explore how racial appeals influence Latino and white political participation. I utilize the U.S. Census Bureau's 1982–2010 Current Population Survey's Voter Supplement, which collects voter data on large samples of racial/ethnic groups, along with the racialization data described in the introduction to examine whether racialized campaign messages influence voter turnout among blacks, Latinos, and whites. Ultimately, the results indicate that racial appeals have no significant influence on turnout for blacks or whites. Latinos, however, are significantly more likely to vote in elections where black candidates make a substantial number of positive racial appeals.

Racialization and Turnout

The Black Electorate

Several political scientists posit that voter turnout will increase when the "cost" of voting decreases. For example, Wolfinger and Rosenstone (1980) argue that if voter registration requirements were removed, U.S. voter turnout would increase by as much as 9 percent. Moreover, Keele and White (2011) show that voter turnout is comparatively low when voters face unfamiliar choices (i.e., when the voters have no experience with the candidate or the candidate has little name recognition). They argue that the cost of learning about new candidates drives down aggregate turnout.[4] In sum, fewer voters turn out as the costs of participation increase.

Black candidates may increase black voter turnout by decreasing costs associated with voting. Many scholars find that a candidate's race, like party affiliation, is used as a voting cue and that blacks often ascribe favorable features to black candidates.[5] Moreover, blacks believe that black elected officials are more responsive to their needs than white officials.[6] As a result, a candidate's race may work as an information shortcut to the candidate's ideology and policy preferences. In essence, for black voters, knowing a candidate shares their race can decrease the cost of learning about an election, and this in turn can increase turnout.

However, not all black candidates equally decrease the cost of voting. It is possible that the cost of participating in an election will be lower for African Americans when black candidates use racial appeals. Holding constant the competitiveness of black candidates, black politicians who make positive and/or negative racial appeals generally garner more media attention than their counterparts. This exposure increases the likelihood that voters will know the candidate's race, which in turn enables black voters to use the candidate's race as a voting cue.

Positive racial appeals also make it easier for black voters to discern which black candidates better represent their policy preferences. Black candidates who run deracialized campaigns still provide a racial cue, but that alone does not guarantee that they will champion issues that concern black voters.[7] Concerns about post-racial black candidates' ability to represent the black community may prompt blacks to learn more about the candidate before they decide to vote for him or her or even vote at all. This extra effort increases the costs of participating in an election and may consequently diminish black candidates' effect on turnout. While negative racial appeals may not provide the same benefits as positive racial appeals, they may be more effective in increasing black turnout because they underscore the candidate's connection to black voters.

In addition to providing a racial cue, black churches and community groups work diligently to mobilize black voters when an African American is on the ballot. These mobilizing efforts have consistently been shown to increase turnout.[8] For example, Preston (1983) partially attributed black Chicagoans' 30 percent increase in turnout in Harold Washington's bid to become Chicago mayor to black organizations' emphasis on registering and mobilizing black voters on his behalf. Tate (1991) arrives at a similar conclusion in examining Jesse Jackson's impact on black political participation in both the 1984 and 1988 Democratic presidential primaries. In particular, she finds that black churches played an instrumental role in mobilizing black voters in support of Jackson's campaign.

Levels of voter mobilization may be tied to beneficial policies for African Americans that candidates' pledge to work for if elected. Black churches and other race-based organizations may be especially active when black candidates outline their agenda for improving the well-being of their community. Moreover, candidates who reach out to the black community are more likely to work with these organizations than post-racial black candidates. For example, Harold Ford Jr. campaigned at several black churches during his 2006 bid for a *Tennessee* U.S. Senate seat. Deracialized 1986 California gubernatorial candidate Tom Bradley, on the other hand, kept his distance from African American activist and PUSH/Rainbow Coalition president Jesse Jackson. Racialized black candidates who work with organizations that advance black political interests may benefit most from these organizations' mobilization efforts.

While the use of racial appeals can increase black voter turnout, black voters may not always respond positively to black candidates' outreach to the black community. In fact, some black voters are alienated by black candidates who make race-based appeals. A number of studies show that voters of all races reject the explicit injection of race into an election because these actions violate the growing norm of a color-blind or "post-racial" society.[9] As a result, black candidates who inject race into a campaign may be perceived as undermining this ideal and may alienate some black voters. This is particularly true of negative racial appeals. Black candidates who inject race into a campaign in a blame-based or attack manner may alienate black voters, as they may perceive them to be creating racial divisions for their own gain.

In addition, black voters may also be less enthusiastic about racialized black candidates because they may perceive them as unelectable. A wave of racialized candidates, from Democratic presidential primary candidate Jesse Jackson in 1984 to Democratic presidential primary candidate Al Sharpton in 2004, failed in their bids for elected office. However, a number of race-neutral candidates, including Obama and Massachusetts governor Deval Patrick succeeded in their bids for high-profile elected offices. It is possible that black voters take the campaigns of racialized black candidates less seriously and are less motivated to turn out for what they perceive as a losing effort. Stout (2010) demonstrates that black candidates who perform better in the polls generally motivate higher levels of black turnout. He attributes this change in turnout to viable black candidates generating more interest and enthusiasm from the black community than their counterparts who are predicted to lose by large margins. Overall, blacks may consider deracialized black candidates as more credible, and this in turn may prompt higher levels of black turnout.

If perceptions of electability matter to voters, it follows that negative racial appeals may deter blacks from voting. Negative racial appeals can often appear to be desperate attacks by frustrated politicians to gain black votes. As discussed in the previous chapter, 1990 South Carolina gubernatorial candidate Theo Mitchell injected race into the campaign by attacking other black politicians for not supporting his candidacy. Mitchell's race-based attacks underscored his struggle for support in the black community, and political analysts claimed it led voters—black, white and Latino—to abandon his campaign.[10] Given that negative racial appeals may signal the candidate's desperation and frustration, these appeals may have a particularly demobilizing effect on black turnout.

The White Electorate

While previous research is mixed about whether white voter turnout increases when black candidates are on the ballot, less is known about how black candidates' racial campaign strategies influence the white electorate.[11] There are a number of reasons why white turnout may increase when black candidates employ a racialized campaign approach. White voters may be motivated to turn out by fears that racialized black candidates will represent

African American interests at the expense of their own.[12] While deracialized black candidates may assuage these concerns in their campaign rhetoric, candidates who campaign using a racialized approach may incite white fears of racial favoritism or reverse racism. Moreover, negative racial appeals can create a sense of divisiveness, an "us vs. them" mentality, which may mobilize some white voters. Taken together, a candidate's consistent use of racial appeals, and particularly negative racial appeals, may increase white voter turnout.

Studies also show a link between political threat from black candidates, mobilization, and voter turnout. Black candidates may increase white turnout when whites perceive black candidates as a threat to the white political hegemony.[13] One of the strengths of a deracialized campaign is that it minimizes perceived differences between black candidates and mainstream white politicians.[14] As a result, post-racial black candidates may neutralize fears of a racial threat and prevent the mobilization of unsympathetic white voters.

It is crucial to note that the white electorate is less monolithic than the black vote. While some whites may be motivated to vote against black candidates who use racial appeals, other whites may be less likely to turn out when a racialized black candidate is on the ballot. Like African Americans, whites who are supportive of black candidates may be less enthusiastic about their candidacies if they are perceived as being unelectable. Given that deracialized black candidates have enjoyed the most electoral success in recent elections, some whites may be discouraged when their party is represented by a racialized black candidate. This feeling of despair or alienation may lead them to skip voting. If a candidate's electability is a key predictor of white turnout, negative racial appeals may dampen white political participation to a greater degree than positive racial appeals. As discussed earlier, negative racial appeals are often associated with black candidates who want to make drastic changes to the political landscape because of their poor electoral standing.

Black candidates who use negative racial appeals may also alienate white voters who feel frustrated by campaigns where racial divisions are highlighted. Ansolabehere et al. (1994) demonstrate that negative television campaign advertisements—those that attack the opponent personally—decrease turnout. The authors argue that some potential voters become disillusioned about politics when candidates focus less on the issues and more on attacking their opponents. This dissatisfaction may discourage voter turnout. Along the same lines, Kahn and Kenney (1999) find that the most egregious forms of personal attacks—those which are perceived as being unsubstantial—deter individuals from voting. Given that negative racial appeals generally constitute egregious personal attacks, it follows logically that black candidates who make racially divisive statements may also depress white turnout. Overall, there is evidence which suggests that racialized black candidates have the ability to increase or to diminish white voter turnout.

The Latino Electorate

The racial tone of the campaign may also influence Latino political participation. Race-neutral black candidates, in an attempt to appeal to white voters, often minimize their connections to all minority groups.[15] For example, Barreto et al. (2008) note that Barack Obama's outreach to Latinos in the 2008 Democratic primaries was weak. As a result, Latino voters were less enthusiastic about his campaign and supported his opponent, Hillary Clinton. Conversely, racialized black candidates may focus more of their attention on mobilizing Latinos. Most famously, Jesse Jackson did this in his first presidential bid. For example, in his 1984 presidential announcement speech, Jackson noted that "Reagan won Illinois by 300,000 votes—800,000 unregistered blacks, 500,000 Hispanics, rocks just laying around. . . . Pick up your slingshot, pick up your rock, and declare [that] our time has come, a new day has begun!"[16] Jackson's appeal reflects his intention of mobilizing black and Latino voters. Racialized politicians such as 2002 Texas U.S. Senate candidate Ron Kirk also focused on mobilizing the Latino community by touting his party's Latino gubernatorial nominee in 2002. Racialized black candidates may increase Latino turnout through their pan-minority mobilizing efforts.

While there are reasons to believe that racialized black candidates can mobilize Latino voters to a greater degree than their race-neutral counterparts, other factors suggest that racialization reduces Latino turnout. A number of studies show that Latinos, like whites, perceive that black candidates pose a major source of political and economic competition and may be less enthusiastic about black candidates whom they perceive as favoring the black community; this too may diminish Latino turnout.[17] Moreover, in a number of polls, Latinos say that they feel closer to whites than they do to blacks.[18] Latinos may be more willing to turn out to support a black candidate who shares their party affiliation if the candidate can minimize perceived racial differences between himself and Latinos by not focusing on issues that concern the black electorate.

Results: Racialization and Turnout

This chapter identifies which type of black candidates—those who use a racialized (positive vs. negative) or race-neutral approach—have the largest impact on mobilizing all voters and the black electorate in particular. To examine this relationship, I utilize the U.S. Census Bureau's 1982–2010 Current Population Survey Voter Supplement,[19] which collects voter data on U.S. racial/ethnic groups' voting patterns and trends. In November of each election year, the U.S. Census Bureau produces a supplemental survey that asks over 100,000 American adults about their voting habits through personal and telephone interviews.[20] While the Current Population Survey works well for this study, it is certainly not without its shortcomings, namely its lack of partisan identifiers, its reliance on self-reported voting behavior, and the fact that it does not differentiate between the political offices that the voters participated in (e.g., a respondent may vote for president, but abstain from voting for county clerk).

The self-reported measures of turnout are particularly concerning as a long line of literature demonstrates that survey respondents are much more likely to overstate whether they participated in an election to appear more politically active.[21] Moreover, research shows that black voters are particularly likely to over-report voting in elections with black candidates.[22] While respondents' over-reporting their political participation rates may raise some reasons for concern, they are not prohibitive for this study for several reasons.

First, some research argues that the over-reporting of voting in most surveys is not as large a problem for understanding voting patterns as some have suggested.[23] Second, research shows that the Current Population Survey often has fewer problems with voters overstating their voting records than comparable surveys.[24] Third, given that I am using the same survey to make comparisons across all cases, the problem of voters over-reporting their turnout should not be systematically greater in one election with a black candidate than another.[25] Thus the comparisons of the Current Population Survey across different elections with black candidates should not largely bias my results. Nonetheless, given that voter turnout is my dependent variable and it is possible that a portion of voters may provide misleading responses regarding their participation rate, it is worth noting this potential pitfall.

While the Current Population Survey is not without its problems, it has a number of strengths that make it appropriate for this analysis. In particular, the data set's inclusion of a number of important variables including political participation measures (e.g., voting and registration information) and racial identifiers and the Current Population Survey's large and diverse sample size makes it a strong data set to examine voting behavior.[26] Using a combination of the Current Population Survey data and the racialization measures described in the introduction, I investigate how racial appeals influence voter turnout.[27]

The voting measure in the CPS Voter Supplement and the content-coded measures for positive and negative racialization were used to create scatter-plots, shown in figures 1 and 2. These figures illustrate the average levels of turnout for (A) black, (B) white, and (C) Latino voters for presidential and nonpresidential elections between 1982 and 2010 plotted against the candidates' positive and negative racialization scores. Both figures include a best fitting line (i.e., a line that minimizes squared differences between itself and all points on the scatterplot) to better illustrate the relationship between turnout and racialization.

Figure 1 reveals a mixed relationship between black candidates' use of positive racial appeals and political participation. Figure 1A shows that a weak association exists between black candidates' positive racialization scores and black voter turnout for both presidential and midterm elections. During presidential elections, black turnout declines precipitously the more black candidates make positive racial appeals. Conversely, during midterm elections, the relationship between positive forms of racialization and black turnout is positive, but the trajectory is extremely flat, indicating a weak relationship between the two variables.

Figure 1B, which includes only white voters, shows a negative relationship between black candidates' use of positive racial appeals and white turnout for both presidential and midterm elections. In both types of elections, white voter turnout decreases by almost 10 percent when black candidates who use the most positive racial appeals are on the ballot. Finally, figure 1C demonstrates that political participation in the Latino community grows with an increase in positive racial appeals during presidential elections, but the same relationship is associated with a decline in voter turnout in other years. Overall, the results suggest that black candidates' use of positive racial appeals do not consistently influence turnout for Latinos voters. These preliminary results also suggest that positive racial appeals may actually decrease white turnout and in some cases black turnout.

Figure 2 displays average levels of voter turnout for different racial/ethnic groups contrasted with negative racial appeals made by black candidates. Figure 2A shows results for black respondents, figure 2B for white respondents, and figure 2C for Latino respondents. Unlike positive racial appeals, negative racial appeals are much rarer. Slightly over half of the black candidates in this analysis did not make any negative racial appeals. In fact, only seven black candidates in my sample were coded as making negative racial appeals in more than two newspaper articles.[28]

As with positive racial appeals, there does not appear to be a consistent pattern based on the scatterplots. For blacks, negative racialization leads to a

FIGURE 1. Average levels of black, white, and Latino turnout and positive racialization

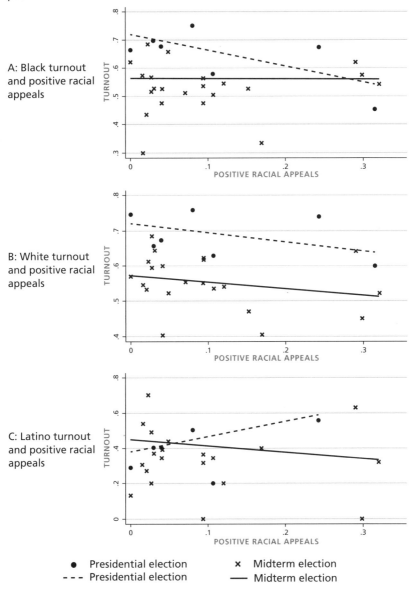

A: Black turnout and positive racial appeals

B: White turnout and positive racial appeals

C: Latino turnout and positive racial appeals

● Presidential election   ✕ Midterm election
- - - Presidential election   —— Midterm election

Source: 1982–2010 Current Population Survey. Lines minimize the squared differences between all points on the graph. The points and lines are disaggregated by midterm and presidential elections. See table 14 in the appendix for the data used to construct these figures.

FIGURE 2. Average levels of black, white, and Latino turnout and negative racialization

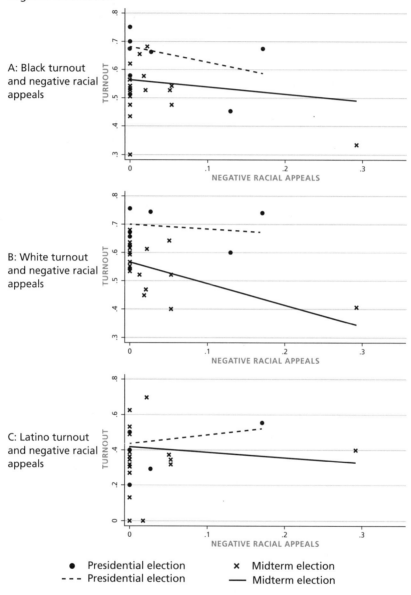

A: Black turnout and negative racial appeals

B: White turnout and negative racial appeals

C: Latino turnout and negative racial appeals

● Presidential election   ✕ Midterm election
- - - Presidential election   —— Midterm election

Source: 1982–2010 Current Population Survey. Lines minimize the squared differences between all points on the graph. The points and lines are disaggregated by midterm and presidential elections. See table 14 in the appendix for the data used to construct these figures.

slight decline in voter turnout during midterm elections but larger declines in black turnout during presidential elections. For example, black turnout decreases by over 10 percent when black candidates use the most negative racial appeals in presidential elections. Conversely, black turnout only decreases by about 4 percent under the same conditions during midterm elections. Similarly, increasing levels of negative racial appeals leads to a slight decline in white turnout during midterm elections and a dramatic decrease in white turnout during presidential elections. White turnout decreases by over 20 percent when black candidates use the most negative racial appeals during presidential elections. Latino political participation also declines with an increase in negative forms of racialization during midterm elections, but surprisingly increases under the same conditions in presidential elections.

In sum, there does not appear to be a clear relationship between black candidates' use of negative racial appeals and voter turnout for any of the three racial/ethnic groups examined. The descriptive results presented in figures 1 and 2 suggest that neither positive nor negative forms of racialization affect voter turnout. However, the inconsistent nature of the results, particularly with differences occurring during presidential and midterm elections, indicates that something else may be driving the differences in voting rates. Moreover, this factor may be obscuring the relationship between racial appeals and voter turnout. Thus more work is necessary to isolate the link between these variables.

Regression Results

To further examine the relationship between racial appeals and voter turnout, I estimate several logit regression models predicting whether an individual voted in a black vs. white candidate U.S. Senate or gubernatorial election. A separate model is estimated for each racial/ethnic group with a sufficient number of respondents.[29] The dependent variable for this model is dichotomous and measures whether an individual reported voting in the November election (1) or did not vote (0).

The goal of each model is to assess how positive and negative levels of racialization influence political participation. Thus the independent variables of interest measure the average levels of positive and negative racial appeals for each black candidate as measured by their average newspaper article score for each of these measures. To isolate the influence of racial appeals on turnout, I also include measures that account for the level of positive and negative racialization by each black candidate's white opponent and by the media. To measure the amount of positive racial appeals made by white candidates, I use the same content coding for positive racialization described in the introduction and applied it to white candidates in each article.

While the positive racialization measure for black and white candidates is the same, white candidates rarely, if ever, make divisive racial appeals in the same manner as black candidates. In fact, applying the same negative racialization standard described in the introduction to white candidates yields scores of zero for every white candidate in my sample. This, however, does not mean that white candidates do not inject divisive racial appeals; they do, but in different ways. The negative racialization for white candidates measures whether they implicitly (score of 1 on the negative racialization scale) or explicitly (score of 2 on the negative racialization scale) make race-based attacks on their black opponents using racial-tinged issues (e.g., crime, welfare, affirmative action) or racially coded language (e.g., "us vs. them") (see appendix for detailed coding).

The media racialization measure accounts for how much focus each article devoted to the race of the candidate. Similar to the candidate's racialization measures, the opponent and media racialization scores are also created through the content analysis of newspaper articles and are scored based on whether the article did not mention the candidate's race (0), mentioned the candidate's race in passing (1), or mentioned the candidate's race in more than two paragraphs or discussed race in the headline of the article (2).[30] Similar to the candidate racialization scores, this measure represents the average media racialization score for the sample of articles for each candidate.

The models also assess whether black Democrats affect turnout differently than their Republican counterparts. Given that black voters disproportionately belong to the Democratic Party, it would not be surprising to find that the combination of having the opportunity to support a candidate who shares both your party and your race increases an individual's incentives to vote. The candidate's performance may also influence levels of voter turnout. To this end, all three models include controls for the candidates' viability as measured by the candidates' experience proportional to their opponents',[31] the candidates' fund-raising totals proportional to their opponents',[32] and the candidates' incumbency status (i.e., was the candidate challenging an incumbent).

I also account for the number of articles in which the candidate was only mentioned in one paragraph. The fewer mentions of the candidate in each article, the less likely the newspaper connected their candidacy to race-based appeals. The models also include controls for the decade in which the candidate was on the ballot, the average turnout in the United States in the year of the election, the average turnout level for the state in which the black candidate ran for elected office (in either the midterm or presidential election excluding the election with the black candidate), the alignment

between the candidate's partisanship and the state's partisanship,[33] whether
the candidate was campaigning for the U.S. Senate or the governor's office, and whether the election was held in a southern state.[34] Finally, the
models include individual-level controls for income, age, education, and
gender.[35]

Table 4 displays logit regression results and predicted probabilities for
three separate regression models predicting whether an individual voted.[36]
Again, each model estimates how various factors (e.g., racial appeals, viability, region, party affiliation, etc.) influence political participation for individuals of different racial/ethnic groups. The predicted probabilities examine the
percentage change in an individual's likelihood of voting when the variable of
interest changes from its minimum to its maximum level, holding all other
variables at their mean. For example, a white voter is about 2 percent more
likely to vote in an election where a black candidate uses the most positive
racial appeals than in an election where a black candidate uses no racial appeals, when all other variables are held at their mean score.

According to the results, as presented in table 4, positive racial appeals
have no statistically significant effect on voter turnout for blacks or whites
when accounting for other factors.[37] This suggests that racialized black candidates do not inspire higher levels of black turnout than their nonracialized
counterparts. The results also indicate that black candidates' use of positive
racial appeals do not correlate with a significant electoral backlash among
white voters. Latinos, however, are significantly more likely to vote in elections in which black candidates make a large number of positive racial appeals. All else being equal, Latinos in elections where black candidates make
the most positive racial appeals are 9 percent more likely to turn out than
their counterparts in elections where the black candidate makes no racial appeals. While the positive racial strategy of a black candidate is inconsequential in motivating black and white voters to turn out, it may be an important
ingredient in spurring voting among Latinos.

Similar to positive racial appeals, negative racial appeals appear to have
no substantial effect on black voters. In combination, race-based appeals appear to be an ineffective way for black candidates to increase black turnout.
However, when other factors are accounted for, white voters are significantly
less likely to vote in elections with large levels of negative racial appeals
made by black candidates. In fact, holding all other variables at their mean,
whites were 14 percent less likely to vote in an election with the highest
levels of negative racialization than they were in elections where black candidates abstained from using negative racial appeals. The results indicate that
white voters feel alienated in elections where black candidates inject divisive

racial politics. While white voters are less enthusiastic about elections where negative racialization is high, black candidates who utilize negative racial appeals are neither punished nor rewarded with changes in turnout from either blacks or Latinos.

White candidates' use of positive racial appeals do not significantly influence voter turnout for blacks and whites. However, it does have a positive effect on Latino turnout. Similar to Latinos' reactions to black candidates, Latino voter turnout increases by about 30 percent, holding all other variables at their mean, when white candidates who make the most positive racial appeals are on the ballot. In combination, Latinos appear to be motivated to vote when candidates, either black or white, show their concern or connection to minority voters.

While black turnout seems to be impervious to racial appeals made by black candidates, blacks are less active in elections when white candidates inject race into a campaign in a divisive manner. Holding all other variables at their mean, when white candidates attack their black opponent using either subtle or overt racial messages, an African American's likelihood of voting decreases by almost 40 percent compared with white candidates who refrain from using race-based attacks. The injection of negative race-based attacks by white candidates may be effective in demobilizing their black opponent's most stalwart supporters.

The partisanship of the black candidate also appears to be a strong predictor of turnout among some minority groups. Latinos are significantly more likely to vote when there is a Democratic black candidate on the ballot than when the black candidate is a Republican. In combination with the results for positive racialization, Latinos turnout in black versus white candidate elections appears to be driven by the ideology of the black candidate. Liberal black candidates appear to inspire higher levels of voting among Latinos than conservative black politicians.

The viability of the candidate, as measured by the candidate's fundraising totals proportional to their opponents, has a significant influence on black and Latino turnout. Black and Latino respondents are significantly more likely to vote when the black candidate outraised their opponent. Along these lines, Latinos and whites are less motivated to vote in elections where black candidates are challenging an incumbent. In combination, the results suggest that the influence of descriptive representation on increasing black turnout is largely a function of the candidate's viability, rather than their message. Black candidates who are sacrificial lambs rarely inspire the same levels of mobilization among minorities as their more credible counterparts.

TABLE 4. Logit regression predicting voting for blacks, whites, and Latinos

	Blacks	% change	Whites	% change	Latinos	% change
Black candidate, positive racialization	0.46 (0.53)	4	0.28 (0.39)	2	1.20*** (0.38)	9
Black candidate, negative racialization	−2.80 (2.03)	−20	−1.95*** (0.75)	−14	−1.29 (1.55)	−8
White candidate, positive racialization	4.27 (2.96)	15	1.09 (1.10)	4	7.01*** (1.32)	27
White candidate, negative racialization	−2.91*** (1.03)	−38	−0.24 (0.75)	−3	−3.60* (2.07)	−36
Media racialization	0.10 (0.15)	2	0.49*** (0.14)	−13	1.08 (0.77)	25
Democrat (candidate)	0.15 (0.17)	4	0.01 (0.08)	0	0.14 (0.13)	3
Experience (proportional to opponent)	0.00 (0.00)	0	−0.00 (0.00)	−3	−0.00** (0.00)	−18
Spending (proportional to opponent)	0.34** (0.13)	25	0.06 (0.09)	5	0.32 (0.22)	28
Non-incumbent candidate	−0.12 (0.12)	−3	−0.14* (0.08)	−3	−0.33*** (0.11)	−8
Campaign in southern state	−0.04 (0.17)	−1	−0.02 (0.12)	0	0.01 (0.17)	0
Female (respondent)	0.24*** (0.04)	6	0.04 (0.02)	1	−0.05 (0.10)	−1
Age (respondent)	0.04*** (0.00)	58	0.04*** (0.00)	62	0.05*** (0.00)	69
Income (respondent)	0.36*** (0.05)	34	0.30*** (0.02)	30	0.16*** (0.05)	16
Education (respondent)	0.17*** (0.01)	68	0.23*** (0.01)	79	0.14*** (0.01)	53
Constant	−2.27* (1.31)		6.11*** (1.04)		−3.09* (1.86)	
Observations	6,218		42,442		3,575	
Clusters	29		29		26	

Source: 1982–2010 Current Population Survey. *Significant at .10. **Significant at .05. ***Significant at .01. Robust standard errors in parentheses. The standard errors are clustered for 26–29 unique elections. *Not all variables included in the model are presented above.* Controls for the office for which the candidate was campaigning (i.e., governor vs. U.S. senator), decade (i.e., 1990, 2000), the relationship between the candidate's partisanship and the state's partisan support for the presidential candidate, average turnout for year and for state, and the percentage of time that the candidate was only mentioned once in an article were included in the model but not shown. "Respondent" indicates that these are respondent level attributes rather than attributes of the candidate.

Conclusion

While a number of studies suggest that deracialized black candidates have a difficult time mobilizing black voters,[38] the results of this chapter indicate that racialization does not have a significant effect on voter turnout when accounting for other factors such as political partisanship, viability, and national region. Black candidates who make either positive or negative racial appeals are no more likely to inspire a significant growth in black turnout than their post-racial counterparts. The results suggest that black voters are more concerned with other aspects of the candidate or the campaign when deciding whether to vote. In particular, the results presented in table 4 indicate that some of the mediating factors between black candidates and black turnout are based more on the viability of the candidate than their message with regard to race.

While positive or negative racialized messages do not appear to mobilize black voters, it does not appear to hurt their candidacies with large levels of counter mobilization from white voters. In fact, positive racial appeals may actually mobilize Latino voters who are often more sympathetic to black candidates than to their white counterparts.[39] Thus the use of these appeals may not necessarily harm a black candidate's bid for elected office as some have argued.

Positive and negative racial appeals may not draw black voters to the polls, as the candidates intend. However, this does not preclude the possibility that black candidates' use of racial appeals influences voters' choices and thus their levels of support. By examining the voting behavior of individuals who do turn out at the polls, we can better ascertain whether positive racial appeals increase voter turnout for those who oppose the black candidate and demobilization among potential supporters. This may be especially true of white voters who are more varied in their partisanship and voting patterns. In combination, these two divergent paths may yield the insignificant result displayed in table 4.

Unfortunately, the Current Population Survey does not ask questions about voters' partisanship, and most national polls such as the American National Election Studies and the General Social Survey have too few minority respondents within each state to determine whether black candidates' racialized campaign approach influences Republican and Democratic voters differently. However, if we find that positive racial appeals decrease the white vote for black candidates, we can better understand how racial appeals influence the partisan composition of the electorate. In the following chapter, we assess these possibilities by examining the relationship between racial appeals and vote choice.

3

Racializing and Winning Elections

HOW VOTERS RESPOND TO NEGATIVE AND
POSITIVE RACIAL APPEALS

In the 1990 South Carolina gubernatorial election, black Democrat Theo Mitchell highlighted why his election to the governor's mansion would benefit black voters. He argued that, if he were elected, blacks would no longer play second fiddle to rich white voters in the state. Mitchell also promised that he would raise some taxes to increase education, social, and health spending to address racial and social inequities in South Carolina.[1] While Mitchell made many positive appeals to black voters, he also made a number of racially divisive statements. In particular, he used offensive language to chastise black leaders who supported his opponent, possibly in hopes of altering the trajectory of his candidacy in a state where blacks make up a large segment of the electorate. In all, Mitchell ran a very racially charged campaign. While his focus on race had the potential to mobilize black voters in support of his candidacy, the strategy failed. One poll showed Mitchell had uncharacteristically low levels of support among black voters,[2] which suggests that positive and/or negative racial appeals are not an effective way to reach out to the black community.

Four years later, in 1994, Washington U.S. Senate candidate Ron Sims took the opposite approach. Instead of campaigning on racial issues, he focused on gun control, the environment, and the North American Free Trade Agreement (NAFTA). He was silent for the most part on the issue of race, as was his white opponent, Republican incumbent Slade Gorton. A reporter covering the election for the *Seattle Post-Intelligencer* noted, "Little has been said in this campaign about Sims's African American identity."[3] While Sims approached the issue of race differently than Mitchell, the result was the same. According to a Voter News Service Exit Poll, almost 20 percent of black voters supported his white opponent. Sims's campaign provides anecdotal evidence that black voters may also be less supportive of black candidates who largely ignore race.

The two examples outlined above exemplify the differences found in studies of racialization and black electoral support. One strain of literature argues that black candidates who fail to make race-based appeals are met with lack-luster support from the black community.[4] A second strain of literature suggests that black candidates who de-emphasize race in their campaigns have a greater ability to attract both black and white supporters.[5] The conflicting nature of these results suggests that more analysis is necessary to determine whether the use of either positive or negative racial appeals is preferable to a deracialized campaign strategy in drawing votes from voters of different races/ethnicities.

In this chapter, I investigate the efficacy of positive and/or negative forms of racial appeals by examining twenty-seven black vs. white candidate U.S. Senate and gubernatorial elections from 1982 through 2010. To accomplish this goal, I begin with an examination of how black voters may respond to black candidates who inject race into an election in a positive or negative manner. I also discuss how these different forms of racialization may influence vote choice for Latino and white voters. Following this, I assess which black candidates receive the highest levels of support from different racial/ethnic groups by estimating several logistic regression models. Overall, the results suggest that black voters prefer black candidates who utilize positive racial appeals and that this positive racialization does not lead to a backlash from white or Latino voters as others have suggested. Conversely, I find that when black candidates inject race into a campaign in a negative manner, they lose support among both blacks and whites. In the conclusion, I discuss the implications of these findings for black candidates' opportunities to succeed in majority white settings.

Racialization and Vote Choice

The Black Electorate

It is unclear whether the use of racial appeals increases or decreases black support. In a recent experimental design study, McIlwain and Caliendo (2011) show that black voters are less supportive of black candidates who are perceived as making race-based appeals. They attribute this result to the growing norm of a color-blind society. While previous generations of black voters were supportive of black candidates who focused on racial inequality, a growing number are socialized in an era when race is perceived as being less important. These younger black voters have a more optimistic outlook about racial relations and thus may be less supportive of candidates who highlight racial differences.[6] Black voters may be particularly offended by candidates who inject race into a campaign in a negative, racially divisive way. This may lead to a backlash among blacks who perceive these candidates to be campaigning on racial divisions that they believe no longer exist.

Black voters may also perceive as unelectable those black candidates who campaign almost exclusively on issues facing the black community such as job training, increasing diversity in public education and employment, and racism in majority white electorates. It is certainly possible that lack of perceived viability translates into lower levels of enthusiasm and support from black voters. The 1990 South Carolina gubernatorial candidate Theo Mitchell's focus on race led one reporter to conclude that "when Mitchell failed to appeal for white votes, most Democrats—black and white—began simply ignoring his campaign."[7] Black activist Al Sharpton's 2004 presidential campaign provides another example. While Sharpton ran on a platform of reducing racial disparities in employment, education, and housing, he was stereotyped as only being a "protest" candidate who struggled to appear viable. Tate (2012) finds that black voters and elected officials were wary of supporting Sharpton because of his low probability of success. African American candidates who make negative racial appeals are more susceptible to being perceived as unelectable, as it is likely that these appeals will offend the majority white electorate. As a result, we may find that negative racial appeals lead to lower levels of black support than positive racial appeals.

It is also possible that black candidates who fail to appeal to African Americans may have a more difficult time garnering their support. In Vanderleeuw et al.'s 2004 examination of black mayoral candidate W. W. Herenton's campaign for mayor of Memphis in 1999, they argue that black leaders were divided about whether to support his candidacy despite his lack of focus on racial issues. This division led to weak support from the black community. In previous campaign cycles (1991 and 1995), Herenton made more positive racial appeals by focusing on issues that disproportionately affected the black community and enjoyed higher levels of support from both black leaders and black voters as a result.[8]

Other African American candidates who have de-emphasized race in their campaigns have met similar fates. In his 1990 Georgia gubernatorial bid, former civil rights activist Andrew Young, a three-term Georgia congressman, failed to win the Democratic nomination in part because of weak support from black voters. Young's ties with business elite and his less-than-stellar record with the black community as mayor of Atlanta during the 1980s led to lower than expected levels of support from black Democrats.[9] Mary T. Schmich of the *Chicago Tribune* notes, "Not only did Young fail to win the rural white vote; it appeared . . . that he didn't inspire blacks to go to the polls in huge numbers. A number of prominent blacks, including Atlanta mayor Maynard Jackson, refused to endorse Young. Some argued that, despite his history as a civil rights leader, Young had ignored blacks during his eight years as mayor."[10] Conversely, black candidates who reach out to the black community through the use of race-based appeals, as was the case with Republican Michael Steele in the 2006 Maryland U.S. Senate election, have enjoyed higher than expected levels of black support.[11]

Some black voters may perceive African Americans who minimize discussions about race and distance themselves from the black community as not being racially authentic.[12] For example, several prominent figures in the black community, including Andrew Young and conservative author Shelby Steele, have even claimed that white politicians such as Bill and Hillary Clinton have more in common with the black community than Barack Obama has.[13] Given these and other critiques of race-neutral black politicians, black voters may wonder whether their connection to these candidates is only skin deep. These concerns may lead black voters to question how much the candidate truly cares about the black community and whether the candidate is taking their votes for granted. Finn and Glaser (2010), for example, showed that blacks who did not feel connected to Obama's campaign were significantly less likely to support him in the 2008 Democratic presidential primary. Moreover, blacks may see deracialized African American candidates as looking out for their own interests rather than for those of the black electorate.[14] This perceived selfishness may lead to a backlash. However, black candidates may be able to allay these concerns by highlighting their connection to the black community through the use of either positive or negative racial appeals.

Black candidates who make positive racial appeals may lead black voters to believe that they will be more substantively represented in government if their candidate succeeds. Research shows that a substantial proportion of voters make decisions about who to support based on the candidates' policy preferences (e.g., on welfare, immigration, social spending, defense spending).[15] Moreover, White (2007) shows that black public opinion is influenced by racial cues. In particular, blacks showed more support for the Iraq war and welfare when these issues were explicitly connected to the black community. Accordingly, black candidates who tie their campaigns to issues of concern (e.g., improving inner city schools, supporting affirmative action) may more readily attract support from black voters than candidates who focus on less salient issues.

Finally, black candidates who make negative racial appeals may be able to draw support from sympathetic black voters who perceive racism to be a significant problem in society. Candidates who argue that they are being discriminated against may incite feelings of racial solidarity and create a rally around the candidate effect. These appeals may lead blacks to feel more protective of a member of their racial group, and this may drive up this candidate's support. For example, 2008 Mississippi Democratic U.S. Senate nominee Erik Fleming tried to increase his support in the black community by arguing that his party was not providing him with proper financial support and insinuating that this decision was racially motivated. In this situation, some blacks may have been upset about Fleming's poor treatment and were willing to donate to his campaign. Moreover, some blacks may have found Fleming or candidates like him to be more sympathetic, and this may have increased these candidates' support in the black community. Although Fleming failed in his bid for the U.S. Senate, he did receive high levels of black support.

The White Electorate

Research shows that black candidates who de-emphasize race in their campaigns are better able to garner support from white voters.[16] The deracialized campaign style is effective because it diminishes whites' fears that black candidates will favor members of their own racial group at the expense of others.[17] Lewis-Beck et al. (2009), Piston (2010), and Min Baek and Landau (2011) show that fears of racial favoritism cost Obama support among white Democrats and independents in the 2008 presidential election. Black candidates who symbolically or substantively appeal to the black community run the risk of being perceived as favoring their racial group over others. While black voters may respond positively to race-based appeals made by black candidates, white voters may perceive this outreach as a threat and be less supportive.

Moreover, a number of studies find that white voters reject overtly racially divisive appeals.[18] This line of research argues that race-baiting is no longer acceptable in American politics, as it violates the ideals of a "post-racial" society. As a result, black candidates who make positive and/or negative racial appeals may jeopardize white support. However, negative racial appeals that use race to attack an opponent or political institution without offering any substantive policy proposals may be perceived as particularly egregious to voters. Whites often view these claims as being insincere and as attempting to play the "race card" to gain more support.[19] As a result, claims of racial victimization may be seen as offensive to some whites who view racism as a problem of the past.

While it is possible that black candidates who utilize racial appeals will perform poorly, there is reason to believe that positive and negative racial appeals could increase support among white voters. For example, some white liberal voters may be receptive to positive racial appeals given that most black candidates frame their support for racially tinged policies in a way that is appealing to all voters.[20] Ravi Perry (2011) finds that black candidates can successfully attract both black and white voters by championing racially tinged issues, such as welfare, if they frame the benefits of the policy in a racially transcendent manner. Moreover, positive racial appeals may lead voters to perceive black candidates as being more endearing and genuine. Along these lines, McIlwain and Caliendo (2011) find that white voters in some instances reward minority candidates whom they perceive as being more racially authentic.

Negative racial appeals may also be an effective way to appeal to white voters because they have the potential to damage the reputation of their rivals. Candidates are often punished at the polls if they are thought to be overtly racist. For example, Mendelberg (2001) found that white voters were less likely to support George H. W. Bush when his Willie Horton advertisement was labeled racist. As a result, the use of negative racial appeals may help black candidates diminish the support of their opponents and offer them a relative advantage at the polls.

The Latino Electorate

There are reasons to expect that Latinos voters will respond positively to racial appeals from black candidates similarly to black voters. Several studies find that Latinos and blacks share a number of policy concerns and preferences. In particular, they are much more supportive of candidates who address inequities in income, education, and housing.[21] Moreover, Hero and Preuhs (2009) find that Latino and black advocacy organizations often share similar objectives, including advancing civil rights, increasing spending on education and health care, and ensuring fair housing opportunities. Black candidates who make positive racial appeals may draw significant levels of support from the Latino community because of their progressive policy platforms. Conversely, race-neutral black candidates may have a more difficult time gaining support from Latinos.

Negative racial appeals may also help black candidates with the Latino community. It is possible that Latinos may be receptive to claims of racism by black candidates because they too are much more likely to report feeling discriminated against than whites.[22] Negative racial appeals may be an effective way to draw support from sympathetic Latino voters who fear that racism is a problem in society. Moreover, these appeals may make the candidate more endearing by highlighting common struggles that racial/ethnic minorities face. In combination, negative racial appeals may help increase black candidates' support.

However, it is also possible that Latinos may prefer race-neutral black candidates to those who utilize racial appeals. Johnson, Farrell, and Guinn (1997) find that large segments of the Latino community perceive African Americans as not working as hard as other races. As a result, Latinos may perceive black candidates who appear much different from white candidates as being less capable of holding high-profile elected office. Black candidates who position themselves as race-neutral, to assuage white concerns, may also improve their standing with Latino voters.

Latino voters may also turn their backs on racialized black candidates because of group competition. A number of studies find that Latinos perceive African Americans as political and economic competitors.[23] Black candidates who highlight race in their campaigns may jeopardize support from Latino voters who are concerned that black candidates may, once in office, work to steer resources to blacks over other racial/ethnic groups. Again, race-neutral black candidates may assuage these fears and benefit from higher levels of Latino support as a result.

Vote Choice and Racial Appeals

To examine the relationship between race and vote choice, I utilize the universe of available exit polls in states where a black candidate campaigned for governor or the U.S. Senate between 1982 and 2010. These polls were taken by CBS News (1982–88), Voter News Service (1990–2000), and the National Election Pool Poll (2002–10).[24] Unfortunately, the available data does not include exit polls for every black candidate who campaigned for high-profile statewide office; however, exit poll data were available for twenty-seven of these black candidates. The aggregated exit poll data set benefits this study because it includes a large number of black respondents from each state. This large sample size increases the racial/ethnic diversity within each poll and allows us to better assess variation in vote choice for black voters. The exit polls sampling design also attempts to mirror the demographic characteristics of the population of each state, which provides a more accurate assessment of vote choice than national polls whose samples are based on the nation's demographic characteristics. However, the data from these polls is not without shortcomings. The main problem with the exit polls is that they do not consistently ask the same demographic and political questions across all years and all states. In particular, only some exit polls ask questions about the respondents' level of education and their political ideology (i.e., liberal and conservative leanings). Given the already limited number of elections that are included in this study, I exclude these two variables from the analysis.

Using the state exit polls from 1982 to 2010 and the racialization data discussed in the introduction and chapter 2, figure 3 scatters the electoral support of each black candidate graphed against their positive racialization scores, which is again the average positive racial appeal score across a sample of newspaper articles. Within each graph, the candidates are disaggregated by party, and the three sub-graphs represent average levels of electoral support from (A) black voters, (B) white voters, and (C) Latino voters. The figures also include a best-fitting line to better illustrate the relationship between vote choice and positive forms of racialization. As the amount of positive racial appeals increases for black candidates, so does their support from black voters. Racialized black candidates such as 2002 Texas U.S. Senate candidate Ron Kirk and 2006 Maryland U.S. Senate candidate Michael Steele received higher levels of support from black voters than other black candidates in their party. Surprisingly, I find that when black candidates increase their use of positive racial appeals, they do not experience a backlash from white and Latino voters. If anything, positive racial appeals appear to increase the candidates' support among these nonblack voting groups. The party of the candidate also does not seem to influence the efficacy of these appeals. Even black Republicans who make positive racial appeals receive higher levels of black support than black Republicans who are race-neutral. While black Democrats gain from positive racial appeals from all minority voters, the same appeals from these candidates do not appear to have as strong an effect on increasing white electoral support.

While positive racial appeals appear to help black candidates, negative racial appeals appear to decrease their electoral support among almost all racial/ethnic groups. The unproductive injection of race into the election had the largest effect on white voters. As black candidates increase their use of negative racial appeals, white support for these candidates declines dramatically.[25] Black candidates' use of negative racial appeals only slightly dampened their support from black voters. The results suggest that black candidates need not stay away from all racial appeals, but they need to avoid negative racial appeals as it deters a substantial portion of the electorate. Surprisingly, Latinos appear to respond positively to the use of negative racial appeals. The results in figure 4 may represent a backlash against black candidates who utilize negative racial appeals, or the relationship may be explained by the fact that black candidates who are already losing by large margins feel more comfortable using these tactics. To better isolate the effect of racialization on vote choice, I turn to regression analysis.

FIGURE 3. Black candidate's average electoral support and positive racialization for blacks, whites, and Latinos

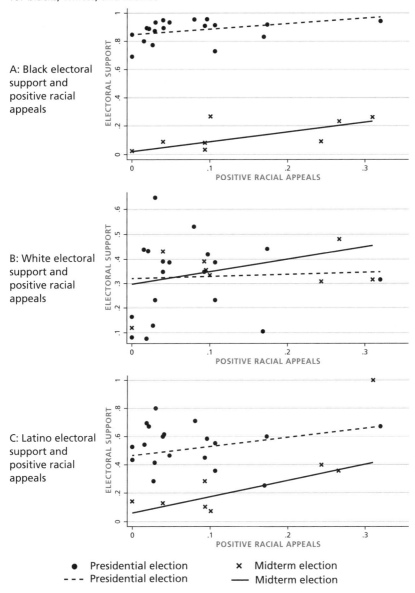

A: Black electoral support and positive racial appeals

B: White electoral support and positive racial appeals

C: Latino electoral support and positive racial appeals

● Presidential election   × Midterm election
- - - Presidential election   —— Midterm election

Source: 1982–2010 State Exit Poll Surveys. Lines minimize the squared differences between all points on the graph. The points and lines are disaggregated for black Democratic and Republican candidates. See table 17 in the appendix for the data used to construct these figures.

FIGURE 4. Black candidate's average electoral support and negative racialization for blacks, whites, and Latinos

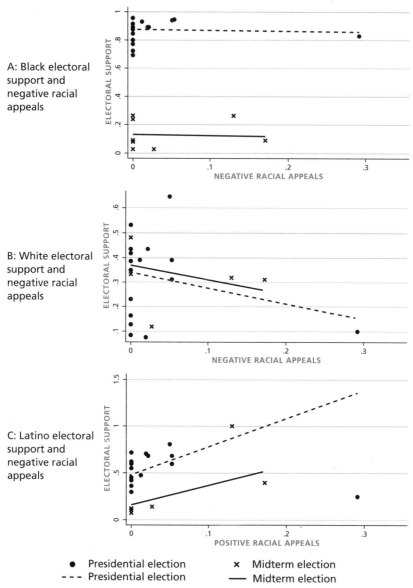

A: Black electoral support and negative racial appeals

B: White electoral support and negative racial appeals

C: Latino electoral support and negative racial appeals

● Presidential election
--- Presidential election
✕ Midterm election
— Midterm election

Source: 1982–2010 State Exit Poll Surveys. Lines minimize the squared differences between all points on the graph. The points and lines are disaggregated for black Democratic and Republican candidates. See table 17 in the appendix for the data used to construct these figures.

Regression Model Results

To assess the effect of different forms of racialization (negative, positive, or neutral) on black candidates' electoral support, I estimate three separate logit regression models to predict whether the respondent from the aforementioned exit polls supported a black candidate or an opponent.[26] Thus the dependent variable is a dichotomous measure that assigns a score of one for those who voted for a black candidate and zero for voters who supported the black candidate's opponent(s).[27] The separate regression models each account for one of the three largest racial/ethnic groups in the United States. Similarly to the estimated models in the previous chapter, these models include measures for positive racialization, negative racialization, and control for the positive and negative injection of race by the black candidate's white opponent and the media's racial coverage.

All three models also control for the viability of the candidates as measured by their amount of monetary support proportional to their opponents, the candidate's incumbency status (i.e., was the black candidate challenging an incumbent), and the black candidate's levels of political experience proportional to their opponent's political experience. The models also account for the partisanship of the candidate, the percentage of the content-coded articles in which the candidate was mentioned only in one paragraph, the decade in which the candidate campaigned for office, whether the candidate was campaigning for governor or U.S. senator, and the region in which the election was held. Finally, the model controls for the partisan congruence between the state's partisanship and the candidate's partisanship.[28]

In addition to context-specific variables, the models also account for variation in the respondent's age, income, gender, and whether the respondent and the black candidates had the same party identification (e.g., a Democratic respondent and a Democratic black candidate).[29] To provide a better understanding of the substantive effect of each variable, I present predicted probabilities derived from the regression equations. These probabilities are created by examining the change in the dependent variable, when the independent variable of interest moves from its minimum value to its maximum value, while all other variables are held at their mean value.

Table 5 presents the results from three separate logit regression models predicting support for black candidates.[30] Each model is run separately for black, white, and Latino respondents. The results shown in table 5 demonstrate that positive forms of racial appeals play a powerful role in shaping black support for co-racial candidates.[31] Black voters are about 29 percent more likely to support black candidates who make the most positive racial appeals than their post-racial counterparts, holding all other variables at their mean. This relationship is statistically significant and holds even when we account for the partisanship of the candidate and his/her viability. Contrary to expectations, positive racialized black candidates' gains from black voters do not dampen their support among whites or Latinos. In fact, Latino voters are marginally more likely to support racialized black candidates than their deracialized counterparts. According to the results presented in table 5, Latinos are 18 percent more likely to support black candidates who utilize the most positive racial appeals than race-neutral black candidates, holding all other variables at their mean score.[32] The results indicate that the use of racial appeals may actually increase black candidates' chances of winning rather than diminish their support as others have suggested.

However, this study finds that negative racial appeals have an adverse effect on black and white support for black candidates. Holding other variables at their mean, white voters are 24 percent less likely to support a black candidate who focuses on negative racial appeals than black candidates who do not use divisive racial rhetoric. Black voters are also significantly less likely to support black candidates who use negative racial appeals; black voters' probability of supporting a black candidate decreases by about 40 percent when black candidates use the most racially divisive rhetoric (i.e., had the highest negative racialization scores). The results suggest that black candidates who utilize negative racial appeals lose the support of almost the entire electorate, regardless of race/ethnicity. Moreover, negative racial appeals have the unintended consequence of dampening support from the crucial black voting bloc.

Contrary to expectations, Latinos voters appear to be more supportive of black candidates when their white opponents make positive racial appeals. This strange result could be attributed to perceptions of the credibility of positive racial appeals made by white candidates in biracial elections. White candidates who make positive racial appeals may not be seen as genuine when their opponent is an African American. As a result, Latino voters may reject white candidates who appeal to minorities in a positive manner in black vs. white candidate elections.

Based on this study's data analysis, white candidates who utilize negative racial appeals also appear to lose the support with some segments of the electorate. Latino voters were significantly less supportive of white candidates who injected race into the campaign in a divisive manner. Moreover, the magnitude of the effect was large. Latinos are about 26 percent more likely to support a black candidate when a white candidate injects the highest levels of divisive racial appeals in an election, holding all other variables at their

TABLE 5. Logit regressions predicting support for black candidates among blacks, whites, and Latinos

	Blacks	% change	Whites	% change	Latinos	% change
Black candidate, positive racialization	7.96*** (2.61)	29	2.06 (1.93)	15	2.23* (1.35)	18
Black candidate, negative racialization	−6.45*** (1.96)	−40	−5.27*** (1.83)	−24	4.54 (4.14)	31
White candidate, positive racialization	1.00 (1.53)	8	0.31 (1.38)	4	7.33** (2.98)	68
White candidate, negative racialization	−1.67 (2.86)	−4	3.36 (2.32)	12	7.01* (4.05)	26
Media racialization	0.42 (0.62)	6	0.96** (0.41)	20	−2.15* (1.16)	−44
Democrat (candidate)	3.79*** (0.42)	73	0.10 (0.23)	2	0.80** (0.32)	19
Experience (proportional to opponent)	0.01 (0.01)	8	0.01 (0.01)	4	0.01 (0.01)	−2
Spending (proportional to opponent)	0.02 (0.27)	1	0.08 (0.19)	6	−0.72* (0.43)	−49
Non-incumbent candidate	−0.12 (0.33)	−2	−0.01 (0.25)	0	−0.12 (0.37)	−3
Democratic support (state)	0.09 (1.27)	1	1.77* (1.01)	22	−0.99 (1.52)	−15
Campaign in southern state	−0.41 (0.28)	−6	−0.10 (0.17)	−2	−0.43 (0.45)	−11
Age (respondent)	−0.01*** (0.00)	−11	−0.01*** (0.00)	−9	−0.00 (0.01)	−6
Female (respondent)	0.04 (0.09)	1	0.09* (0.05)	2	−0.06 (0.10)	−2
Income (respondent)	0.02 (0.03)	2	−0.02 (0.02)	−2	0.01 (0.05)	2
Same party as candidate (respondent)	1.82*** (0.18)	32	2.34*** (0.11)	51	2.19*** (0.19)	50
Constant	−3.52** (1.59)		−3.09** (1.21)		−6.99*** (2.46)	
Observations	6,052		29,146		1,144	
Clusters	27		27		27	

*Significant at .10, **Significant at .05, ***Significant at .01. Results are derived from three separate logit regressions predicting vote choice (voted for a black candidate = 1, did not vote for a black candidate = 0) for each racial/ethnic group. *Not all variables included in the model are presented above.* Controls for the decade in which the candidate campaigned for office, the office for which the candidate was campaigning (i.e., governor vs. U.S. senator), the percentage of times the candidate was only mentioned once in an article was included in the model but not shown. See appendix for full model. "Respondent" indicates that these are respondent level attributes rather than attributes of the candidate.

mean. Surprisingly, black voters are not significantly less likely to support white candidates who make racial attacks than they are white candidates who refrain. The media's racial coverage of the election also had a strong effect on vote choice. Whites were significantly more supportive of black candidates when race was a salient feature of the election. Latinos, however, are less likely to support black candidates in elections where the media coverage focuses on race.

When other factors are accounted for, black and Latino voters are about 73 and 19 percent, respectively, more likely to support a black Democrat over a black Republican. This result is not surprising, as both blacks and Latinos disproportionately belong to the Democratic Party. Surprisingly, Latino voters were less supportive of black candidates who performed well in terms of fund-raising. This odd result may be due to the fact that candidates with fewer resources may focus mostly on appealing to their base, which for black candidates is largely made up of minority voters.

The state context also had a large influence on white support for black candidates. White voters were more supportive of black candidates whose partisanship was not out of step with the state's partisanship. All else being equal, white voters are 20 percent more likely to vote for a black candidate in a state where the candidate's party performs well. But given that blacks and whites have had a tumultuous relationship in the South, it is not surprising to find white southern voters are less supportive of black candidates.

At the individual level, a few factors predict support for black candidates. Older black and white voters (those over age sixty-five) are significantly less likely to support black candidates than their younger counterparts. In fact, the oldest white voters are 7 percent less likely to support black candidates than eighteen-year-olds. The results suggest that as these older voters make up a smaller segment of the population, black candidates may have a greater opportunity to succeed in majority white electorates. Gender is also a significant predictor of black candidate support for white voters. White women are more likely to vote for a black candidate than are white males. This result may be attributed to the fact that women tend to be more liberal and thus more open to supporting a nontraditional candidate than their white male counterparts. The magnitude of the effect for gender, however, is very small (~2%). As expected, voters of all racial/ethnic groups are more likely to support the candidate who shares their partisanship than candidates who do not. The magnitude of this effect is also quite large. For example, whites and Latinos who have the same partisanship as the black candidates are 50 percent more likely to support the candidate than those who are political independents or those who have a party identification that differs from the black candidate.

Conclusion

The results presented in this chapter clearly show that substance—a candidate's stand on issues, particularly issues facing the black community—matters for black voters. Black candidates who reach out to the black community enjoy higher levels of black electoral support than their post-racial black counterparts. This is evidenced by blacks' high levels of support for candidates who make positive racial appeals. Black candidates who outline the benefits they provide to the black electorate or demonstrate their connection to the black community can count on almost unanimous black support. This finding confirms earlier research which suggests that black candidates who take black voters for granted and do not vocally commit to supporting their concerns may be disappointed at the polls.[33] In a slight twist to this argument, race-neutral black candidates don't lose support from black voters because they abstain from voting, as found by some researchers,[34] but because some blacks vote against them.

Contrary to conventional wisdom, black candidates can appeal to the black community without worrying about an electoral backlash from whites. In fact, positive racial appeals may actually help. In particular, black candidates who make positive racial appeals benefit from higher levels of support among Latino voters. As blacks and Latinos share many of the same concerns (e.g., employment and training opportunities, access to quality education and housing, public safety) and reside in very similar neighborhoods, it is not surprising to find that the same campaign tactics that appeal to black voters also appeal to Latinos. As the black and Latino populations continue to grow in the United States, black candidates may find it increasingly advantageous to make positive racial appeals.

The results of this research also provide more support to the claim that positive racial appeals do not lead to countermobilization among racially conservative white voters. Given that the Current Population Survey does not include party identification markers, it was difficult to discern whether the null result between positive racialization and white voter turnout (as reported in the previous chapter) can be explained by lackluster turnout from would-be supporters and a mobilized white opposition. The results from this chapter demonstrate that positive racial appeals do not energize white political opposition to black candidates. Again, this indicates that black candidates can use a positive racial approach without fears of an electoral backlash.

In contrast, negative racial appeals jeopardize support from most voters across racial/ethnic lines. According to the analysis in this chapter, white voters are 24 percent less likely to vote for a black candidate who heavily employed negative racial appeals than their counterparts who avoided this type of rhetoric. Black voters are also less supportive of black candidates who use negative racial appeals. Negative racial appeals may be perceived as black candidates' blaming racism for their lackluster performance rather than taking personal responsibility for their political views and campaign style, along with their experience, skills, and overall electability. Such comments may alienate voters of all races/ethnicities who perceive these black candidates as countering the ideals of a color-blind society. While this strategy may work in some elections contexts, such as those with two black candidates, negative race-based appeals are counterproductive in biracial elections with majority white electorates.

Despite these findings on the advantages of black candidates' use of positive racial appeals, an essential question remains. Why are black candidates who inject race via positive racial appeals into an election less successful than their counterparts who don't? The results in this study indicate that these differences in outcomes may be better explained by something other than how black candidates address the issue of race. Instead, lack of support for black racialized candidates may have more to do with the quality of their opponents or their electoral context, particularly in terms of the partisan makeup of the state. For example, 2004 deracialized Illinois U.S. Senate candidate Barack Obama's opponent, Republican Alan Keyes, did not have substantial political experience and had recently moved to Illinois just to run for the Senate seat. Similarly, Carol Moseley Braun's opponent in the 1992 Illinois U.S. Senate race was Richard Williamson, who had no elected experience. These candidates' good fortune of competing against less experienced opponents may have as much to do with their victory as their deracialized campaign styles.

The differences in outcome may also be attributed to the electoral settings in which these candidates campaign. For example, deracialized black candidate Deval Patrick ran for governor of Massachusetts in 2006, a state where Democrats have a large electoral advantage. Racialized Republican candidate Michael Steele ran in the same year, but faced a less friendly electorate in the Democratic-dominated state of Maryland, and he lost. As with the quality of the opponent, the political context of the election may be a greater barrier to black representation than the candidates' use of positive and negative racial appeals.

Moreover, black candidates who make positive racial appeals are also more likely to make negative racial appeals than their post-racial counterparts. As detailed in the analysis above, negative racial appeals dampen electoral support for black candidates among all voters including African Americans. As a result, the gains made by positive racial appeals may be offset by a candidate's intermittent use of negative racial appeals. The results presented in this chapter suggest that positive racial appeals may be mistakenly blamed for the poor performance of some black candidates when other factors are in fact responsible.

While this chapter demonstrates that blacks and Latinos respond positively to constructive race-based appeals, some critical questions remain. First, does the same relationship between racial appeals and voting behavior hold for candidates who run for elected office outside of the state level? In particular, are high-profile *national* candidates who racialize associated with the same changes in voting patterns as were found with *statewide* candidates in this chapter? Second, do racial appeals truly change voters' minds, or are voters already more or less supportive of black candidates who inject race into the campaign in either a positive or negative manner? Finally, what factors drive the efficacy of positive race-based appeals? In the following chapters, I will address these questions with an examination of black presidential candidates Jesse Jackson and Barack Obama.

4

The First Black President

A COMPARISON OF POLITICAL BEHAVIOR IN THE 1988 AND 2008 DEMOCRATIC PRESIDENTIAL PRIMARIES

In October 1987, Jesse Jackson announced that he would again seek the Democratic nomination for the presidency. Given that Jackson's 1984 presidential campaign had centered on racial issues and was marred by an instance where he used divisive rhetoric, expectations for his 1988 presidential bid were initially very low. However, Jackson changed his strategy in 1988. While his platform was still racial in nature, he focused on issues that were of concern to the black community but also had a broader populist appeal. In 1988, Jackson was no longer the quintessential racial protest candidate. Instead, he was one of several black candidates who championed racially tinged issues, highlighted his association with the black community, and remained competitive for high-profile elected office.

Twenty years later, Barack Obama, a freshman senator from Illinois, announced that he too would seek the Democratic nomination for the presidency. While Jackson ran a campaign that focused on positive racial appeals, Obama ran a much more deracialized campaign. Some pundits even called Obama the "anti–Jesse Jackson" candidate for his ability to back issues that transcend race.[1]

While Jackson and Obama ran vastly different campaigns, the contexts of their elections were remarkably similar. Both were following Republican presidents who were unpopular with Democratic voters. They both ran against accomplished opponents in the primaries who had vast name recognition, and neither Obama nor Jackson enjoyed the ubiquitous support of black or white political elites. They were both household names, and they made widely praised speeches at the Democratic National Convention four years before they were campaigning for president. Both campaigned in primaries that were so competitive it was expected that super-delegates would make the decisive vote at the convention. Most important, both candidates were in the process of making history by attempting to become the first African American nominated by a major party for the presidency. While there are some differences between the two election cycles, there are enough similarities for us to examine how the campaign styles of Jackson and Obama influenced their ability to energize and draw support from black, white, and Latino voters.

The 2008 and 1988 Democratic presidential primaries serve as a good comparison to further investigate the relationship between racialization and electoral behavior. To that end, I examine whether the different campaign styles of Jesse Jackson in 1988 and Barack Obama in 2008 led to a more mobilized electorate in their respective Democratic primaries. Moreover, I test whether the different levels of racialization between the two campaigns yields more or less support from voters of different races/ethnicities. If we find a similar relationship between racialization and electoral behavior with *prominent national* black candidates, we will have more support for the findings presented in chapters 2 and 3, which show that racialized messages increase support for black candidates but have little effect on influencing turnout.

The chapter begins with a detailed review of the Democratic primary campaigns of Jackson in 1988 and Obama in 2008. This review highlights the similar campaign circumstances while detailing the contrary approaches the candidates used to address race. Following this review, I use state exit polls from 1988 and 2008 and the 1988 and 2008 American National Election Study to determine whether either candidate increased turnout or performed better with black, white, and/or Latino voters in the Democratic primary. I conclude with a brief discussion of how the results from this chapter in combination with the results of previous chapters inform us about the electoral connection between black candidates, their campaign styles, and the electorate.

A Positive Racialized Campaign: Jesse Jackson and the 1988 Democratic Primary

In 1984, Jesse Jackson was described as a "protest" candidate with a low probability of success. Jackson's focus on racial issues allowed him to appeal to the black community but made him a single issue/constituency candidate who lacked broader appeal. Over the following four years, he transformed his message and his image to show that he was no longer just a single constituency candidate. Instead, he would work to alleviate the plight of all poor Americans, regardless of race, religion, or creed. One political pundit, Mike Royko, jokingly noted that Jackson's campaign message "now transcends race, ethnicity, social class, age, sexual preference, height, weight, shoe size, and possibly the most distant galaxies of outer space."[2] Instead of highlighting racial differences, Jackson's campaign focused on creating a rainbow coalition of all voters. Jesse Jackson Jr. noted that his father was the only candidate who had a "real commitment to lifting the common lot of poor people."[3]

While Jackson did not highlight racial differences in 1988, his campaign was centered on racially tinged issues. For example, Jackson said that he would reverse the amount of defense spending that grew precipitously under President Ronald Reagan and reallocate those resources to social programs that address education, homelessness, and drug problems in urban areas. Jackson also advocated for increased funding for federal college student aid so that tuition was no longer a barrier to capable college students who could not afford to attend. In terms of social spending, Jackson advocated for an expansion of Medicaid, increasing the number of programs that feed the poor, increasing federal subsidies for child care, and reversing the Reagan administration's changes to federal housing programs. All of these proposals disproportionately affect blacks but could draw support from voters of all races.

While his campaign focused on issues that were not explicitly racial, Jackson would often make overt racial appeals to the black community. Jackson justified his tough position on drugs, for example, by arguing that the drug epidemic in poor neighborhoods was hurting African Americans. He equated the drug problem to the Ku Klux Klan because both devastated the black community. "They aren't wearing hoods, they are hoods," Jackson said of drug traffickers. He added that drugs were more harmful to the black community than lynching: "We've lost more to dope than we have to the rope."[4] Jackson also appealed to black voters by highlighting that he was the only presidential candidate who devoted attention to the plight of blacks in Africa. Jackson was a strong proponent of increasing economic sanctions on South Africa in protest of apartheid. Moreover, Jackson made numerous appearances at black churches and spoke at several NAACP chapters in attempts to mobilize black voters. In all, Jackson ran a campaign that made numerous high-profile positive racial appeals.

Context: The 1988 Campaign

After eight years of a Republican in the White House, Democratic voters were very excited to have the opportunity to elect a Democrat. Ronald Reagan, who once was very popular with Democrats, fell out of favor as the economy began to lag and ethics questions arose about his administration's covert support of rebels in Central America. Moreover, a rising budget deficit caused by increased military spending and lower tax revenues angered many voters. The combination of these factors made the Republican Party very vulnerable in 1988. Frustrations with the Reagan administration and the favorable electoral context led Democratic voters to yearn for a more liberal candidate. While Democrats agreed that they wanted to nominate the anti-Reagan candidate, they disagreed about who that candidate should be.

Many expected that 1984 Democratic presidential primary candidate Colorado U.S. senator Gary Hart would be the nominee. However, he decided not to run for president after personal scandals soured his public approval ratings. Others believed that Arkansas governor Bill Clinton, who enjoyed high levels of public support in his state, would run. However, he too declined. In the end, a number of prominent and well qualified candidates entered the race. Massachusetts governor Michael Dukakis, Missouri congressman Dick Gephardt, Tennessee U.S. senator Al Gore, Illinois U.S. senator Paul Simon, and civil rights activist Jesse Jackson were among the most notable.

Most people had low expectations for Jackson's 1988 bid. He performed very poorly in a previous presidential campaign four years earlier and did not have any elected experience. More important, many expected that Jackson would again run a "protest" campaign whose message would not resonate with white voters. While Jackson was predicted to perform poorly, his better than expected finishes in both Iowa and New Hampshire improved perceptions of his candidacy. Jackson's ability to receive almost double digit support in Iowa, a state where blacks make up only 1 percent of the population, showed that Jackson's message appealed to more than just black voters. Jackson did not secure a victory in any of the first five state primaries or caucuses, but his better than expected performance led some to believe that he could actually win. Increased optimism in Jesse Jackson's electability led people to take his candidacy more seriously.

Jackson's ability to survive in the early primary states, which were predominately made up of white voters, improved his electoral outlook. On Super Tuesday, several southern states with large black electorates would decide who they wanted to be the Democratic nominee. While Jackson was heavily outspent by Dukakis and Gore, he was one of the big winners on Super Tuesday. Jackson won five of the sixteen primaries held on that date. Even more impressive was that Jackson was able to garner about 12 percent of the white vote in these states. The combination of Jackson's success and the dismal performances of some of his opponents catapulted him into the top tier of presidential candidates.

Following his success on Super Tuesday, Jackson put together a string of impressive victories. Not only did he win big in South Carolina, but he was able to secure a victory in predominately white Alaska. His populist message appealed to Democratic voters in the state as their economy was hit hard by a decline in oil prices. Jackson followed his success in Alaska by posing a strong challenge to Paul Simon in their home state of Illinois. Following the Illinois primary, Jackson had the second most delegates, and many political pundits who had disregarded his candidacy now focused on what could happen should he become the nominee.

Following Illinois, Michigan was the next important primary state. While Jackson had momentum on his side, Dukakis won a number of high-profile endorsements in the state, including one from the black mayor of Detroit, Coleman Young. Young said that he did not mean to hurt Jackson's campaign, but he questioned Jackson's electability in the general election.[5] Despite Young's lack of support, Jackson surprised many political pundits and defeated both Dukakis and Gore in Michigan. The result made him not only a serious contender but also the frontrunner.

Scrambling to combat Jackson's surging campaign, Dukakis and Gore focused on New York. Given Jackson's frontrunner status, his opponents highlighted his past indiscretions, including his trips to Libya and Cuba to meet with controversial leaders Moammar Gaddafi and Fidel Castro in attempts to bring prisoners home. Moreover, some began to question Jackson's relationship with the Jewish community, an important voting bloc in New York. In particular, the controversy surrounding anti-Semitic comments that Jackson made in his 1984 presidential bid received a lot of attention.[6] To make matters worse, New York mayor Ed Koch argued that Jews would have to be crazy to support Jackson.[7] Jackson fought back by appealing to Jewish voters: "The sons and daughters of the Holocaust must find common ground with the sons and daughters of slaves."[8] He also argued that Koch and others were being divisive to mask the true problems facing Americans. Despite these appeals, he was defeated in New York by Dukakis.

Jackson's consecutive defeats in New York, Wisconsin, Pennsylvania, Indiana, and Ohio gave Dukakis the numerical majority needed to capture the nomination. Jackson continued to compete, but after defeats in Ohio and Indiana his candidacy was largely symbolic. While Jackson was not successful in his bid to be president, his campaign played a large role in influencing the Democratic Party's platform in 1988. Moreover, it laid the foundation for future black politicians. As Jackson's campaign manager, Willie Brown, prophetically told the *Christian Science Monitor*, "Jackson has opened up doors that black folk probably would not have seen opened prior to the turn of the century. Before the end of this century, there will be blacks running for governors, for U.S. senators, and getting elected."[9]

A Post-Racial Campaign: Barack Obama and the 2008 Democratic Presidential Primary

Obama took a markedly different approach to campaigning. He not only shied away from racial topics but he also campaigned on issues that were not salient in the black community. In particular, he focused on ending the war in Iraq and diverting resources to the war in Afghanistan. Moreover, like his rivals, he advocated for a national health care plan. However, unlike his rivals, Obama's initial plan failed to cover all Americans. While Jesse Jackson advocated for the most socially progressive policies, Obama's campaign was more moderate. Obama also focused on increasing federal spending for a stimulus program to help the ailing economy and for middle-class tax cuts. While Obama was a left-of-center candidate, his campaign was not remarkably different from any his Democratic primary opponents. In fact, some have argued that his campaign was more out of sync with the black community than some of his Democratic rivals.[10]

While Obama shied away from racial issues, his opponents injected race into the campaign at several junctures. For example, Bill Clinton argued that Obama's win in South Carolina was unimpressive because Jesse Jackson had won the predominately black state both in 1984 and 1988.[11] One of Clinton's supporters, former vice presidential candidate Geraldine Ferraro, mentioned that Obama would not be the nominee if he were not black.[12] Despite most of these comments, Obama was able to remain above the fray and continue to campaign on race-neutral policies.

Obama's nonracial campaign strategy was threatened, however, with the discovery of controversial statements made by his preacher. Obama's pastor. Jeremiah Wright made a number of contentious comments during sermons, including blaming America's foreign policy for the September 11 attacks, saying, "Chickens are coming home to roost." In another sermon, Wright argued that America's history of slavery and human rights abuses would eventually catch up with the United States.[13] Obama quickly denounced the comments, but the controversy did not subside. In a March 18, 2008, speech titled "A More Perfect Union," which will be discussed in more detail in the following chapter. In the speech, Obama addressed the complexities of race in the United States. He argued that the nation has made significant strides toward erasing racial prejudices, but that the legacies of racism are still prevalent. While the speech highlighted the reality of racial disparities in the United States, it stopped short of advocating for policies that would address these inequities.

While the More Perfect Union speech highlight Obama's thoughts about racial disparities in the United States, outside of the speech (which occurred late in the 2008 Democratic Primary season), Obama's lack of focus on racial issues and his black identity drew the ire of some black leaders. Obama declined to speak at the State of the Black Union in February 2008, which frustrated prominent figures including Tavis Smiley and Al Sharpton.[14] In an unrelated incident, Jesse Jackson was caught saying that Obama speaks down to black people.[15] While Obama's opponents and the media focused on injecting race into the campaign, Obama was able to run a campaign that was mostly devoid of race-based appeals.

Context: The 2008 Campaign

After eight years in the White House, Republican president George W. Bush had very low approval ratings. Like Reagan before him, Bush had cut taxes and increased military spending, leading to soaring budget deficits. Also, like the Reagan administration, Bush's staff was charged with several ethics violations including the vice president's chief of staff outing a CIA operative. Bush's poor performance and Americans' frustrations with the Iraq war gave progressives the upper hand in the 2008 election. This in combination with an opportunity to reclaim the White House energized Democratic voters. As was the case in 1988, Democrats wanted a candidate who was going to represent the liberal wing of the party.

Many expected that this candidate would be the two-term U.S. senator from New York and former First Lady, Hillary Rodham Clinton. Clinton was mentioned as a possible contender in 2004, but waited to run until 2008. While Clinton was mulling over her decision to run for president, a black state senator was beginning his meteoric rise to the White House. Most of the nation was introduced to Barack Obama when he gave a stirring speech at the 2004 Democratic National Convention. Given his performance at the convention and the large role he played in campaigning for other Democratic candidates in 2006, few were surprised when he decided to run for president.

Like Jesse Jackson, many voters were excited about Obama, but questioned his ability to win the nomination. Obama had only served in the U.S. Senate for three years and was challenging Hillary Clinton, who had the support of most of the Democratic elite. Obama's first test came in the state of Iowa, where he devoted a lot of time and resources. His attentiveness to Iowa paid large dividends, as Obama was able to defeat Clinton in the predominately white state. This led many to believe that Obama's race would not be a significant barrier to his success.

His luck changed in New Hampshire. Clinton appeared vulnerable. Although Obama was leading in most pre-election polls, and Clinton seemed vulnerable, she defeated him. Her victory in New Hampshire coupled with a win in the Nevada caucuses allowed her to regain her status as the front-runner.

There was one election left before Super Tuesday, and this was to be held in South Carolina, a state in which blacks made up a majority of primary voters. Hillary and Bill Clinton heightened their criticism of Obama's antiwar policies and his health care plan going into the South Carolina primary. A third consecutive defeat for Obama in a state that was predominately black would derail his campaign. The negativity of Clinton's message backfired. Not only was she defeated in South Carolina, but her attacks on Obama led a number of Democratic elected officials, including Ted Kennedy, to endorse Obama before the critical Super Tuesday primaries.[16]

While Clinton outperformed Obama on Super Tuesday, including winning the popular vote in large states such as California, New York, and Massachusetts, the proportional division of delegates allowed Obama to remain competitive. Clinton's campaign invested heavily in defeating whoever their opponent would be by Super Tuesday. Thus her campaign had less cash on hand and had poorer organizations in the post-Super Tuesday states. The fact that Obama remained competitive put Clinton at a disadvantage. Following Super Tuesday, Obama won ten consecutive contests, including primaries in Virginia and Wisconsin. The Clinton campaign was able to win in Ohio and Texas in early March, and later in Indiana and Pennsylvania, but she was not able to win by large enough margins to overcome Obama's delegate advantage. Clinton officially ended her presidential bid on June 7, 2008. With Clinton's resignation, Obama became the first African American to be nominated by a major party for the office of president.

Do the Different Campaign Styles Influence Vote Choice or Turnout?

To assess whether the dissimilar campaign styles of Jesse Jackson and Barack Obama had a differential impact on turnout and electoral support, I utilize two sets of surveys. The first set is primary state exit polls that were collected after each state's presidential primary in 1988 and 2008. The 1988 primary state exit polls were collected by CBS in collaboration with the *New York Times*. The 2008 primary state exit polls were conducted by another group including CNN, ABC, and CBS. I use these polls to estimate vote choice in the Democratic presidential primaries. The polls have the advantage of not only having a large number of respondents of all races, but are also weighted to mirror the actual state population. The large, diverse sample size provides for greater variation in vote choice among individuals of different races/ethnicities, which allows for a more nuanced assessment of voters' preferences.

Unfortunately, exit polls do not record information on nonvoters. To assess voter turnout in the two elections, I turn to the 1988 and 2008 American National Election Studies (ANES). In both years, the surveys ask respondents whether they voted in the presidential primaries. The 1988 and 2008 ANES provide the perfect opportunity to determine whether black and white voter turnout was influenced differently by the campaigns of Jesse Jackson and Barack Obama.[17]

TABLE 6. Black, white, and Latino Democratic voter turnout in 1988 and 2008 Democratic presidential primaries

	N	Jackson 1988 (percent)	N	Obama 2008 (percent)	Difference (Jackson–Obama; percent)
Black	164	51	403	52	−1
White	507	44	429	53	−9*
Latino			227	48	

Source: 1988 and 2008 American National Election Study. *Significant at .05. Test of means assesses whether Democratic respondents were more or less likely to vote in the 1988 or 2008 Democratic presidential primaries. Too few Latinos were surveyed in 1988 to draw any conclusions about this population.

Table 6 displays the percentage of Democrats who voted in the 1988 and 2008 Democratic presidential primaries by race/ethnicity.[18] African Americans turned out at similar rates both in 2008 and 1988. More than half of eligible African Americans voted when Barack Obama or Jesse Jackson was on the ballot.[19] The results suggest that Jackson, the more racialized black candidate, was not able to mobilize black voters more than Obama, the post-racial black candidate. These results provide more evidence that black candidates who utilize positive racial appeals are not able to mobilize African Americans to a greater degree than their deracialized counterparts. While black turnout did not differ between 1988 and 2008, the presence of a black candidate boosted black turnout relative to whites who generally possess socio-demographic characteristics (e.g., higher socioeconomic status) that make them more likely to vote. In fact, black turnout exceeded that of white voters in 1988 by more than 7 percent.

White Democratic turnout in the 2008 primaries significantly exceeded white turnout twenty years earlier. It rose from 44 percent in 1988 to 53 percent in 2008. The 9 percent difference in turnout is statistically significant at .05. The result may suggest that Jackson's racialized rhetoric alienated some white Democratic voters. However, the result may also be attributed to the large amount of money spent by the 2008 presidential candidates to mobilize voters. Also, whites may have turned out at higher rates in 2008 because they were more excited about the candidates than they had been in 1988. While most Democrats were enthusiastic about both Hillary Clinton and Barack Obama, many felt that the 1988 presidential candidates were less exciting. For example, former New York governor Mario Cuomo made a joke in 1988 in which a mugger seizes a Democratic voter in Central Park, puts a knife to his throat, and asks, "Which is it: Dukakis, Jackson, or Gore?" "Go ahead and kill me," replies the victim.[20]

While there are too few eligible Latino voters in the 1988 ANES to draw inferences about their participation rates, in 2008 it appears that a substantial portion of the Latino community voted when Clinton and Obama battled for the nomination. Almost half of Latino Democrats voted in the 2008 Democratic presidential primaries. While Latinos generally lag far behind whites and blacks in terms of voting rates, the 2008 election appeared in some ways to erase racial/ethnic disparities in turnout.

Table 7 presents the levels of electoral support for black candidates among black, white, and Latino voters in 1988 and 2008. These results are derived from 1988 and 2008 primary state exit polls. In both elections, the race of the respondent played a large role in predicting vote choice. Black voters overwhelmingly supported both Jesse Jackson and Barack Obama over their Democratic rivals.[21] Conversely, a majority of white Democrats voted for a white candidate rather than support either of the two leading black candidates. Latino voters were less supportive of Obama in 2008 than blacks, but equally as supportive as whites.

Blacks were not more likely to turn out in 1988 than they were in 2008, but those who did vote were more likely to support Jackson than Obama. Jackson received 92 percent of the black vote and 7 percent more of the black vote than Obama. This difference is not only substantial in size but also statistically significant. As shown in chapter 2 with black U.S. Senate and gubernatorial candidates, black voters appear to prefer black candidates who provide more than just pure racial representation. Thus to maximize support in the black community, black candidates should devote more time and effort appealing to black voters.

White voters were much more likely to support the deracialized candidate, Obama, than Jackson. While over a third of white voters supported Obama in 2008, only 11 percent supported Jackson in 1988. This difference in white support of over 25 percent, explains why Obama succeeded and Jackson did

TABLE 7. Black, white, and Latino electoral support for Jesse Jackson in 1988 and Barack Obama in 2008

	N	Jackson 1988 (percent)	N	Obama 2008 (percent)	Difference (Jackson–Obama; percent)
Black	7,319	92	7,725	85	7*
White	27,828	11	26,635	38	−27*
Latino	608	31	2,236	38	−7*

Source: 1988 and 2008 state exit polls. *Significant at .05. Test of means assesses whether black, white, or Latino respondents were more or less likely to support Jesse Jackson rather than Barack Obama.

not. Latinos, too, preferred Obama to his more racialized counterpart. Latino support for Obama was 7 percent greater than it was for Jackson twenty years earlier. Again, this result was statistically significant. Unlike the deracialized statewide candidates, the use of positive racial appeals by Jackson appears to hurt his standing among nonblack voters.

Conclusion

There are a number of corollaries between Jesse Jackson's 1988 presidential campaign and Barack Obama's 2008 bid for the White House. However, there are some differences. The largest difference between the two candidates was how they approached race. Obama focused on issues that transcended race, such as the war in Iraq, health care, and foreign policy. Conversely, Jesse Jackson focused much of his attention on issues that were important to the black community, including the drug epidemic and increasing social spending to address growing inequities between the rich and the poor. The similar contexts in combination with the different campaign styles provided the opportunity to examine whether black voters preferred one candidate's campaign style over another in a very high-profile setting.

Jackson and Obama have played an important role in advancing black politics. Both were able to incorporate black voters by bringing them to the polls and by showing younger African Americans that they too could compete for the highest political office in the United States. While black voters were overwhelmingly supportive of both candidates and turned out in equal numbers in 1988 and 2008, blacks preferred Jackson over Obama. This result corroborates the findings in the previous chapter, which examined black U.S. Senate and gubernatorial candidates in an election setting that generates higher levels of interest. Even in presidential primaries, when the partisanship of the candidate is held constant, it appears that black voters have a preference for candidates who campaign on issues that are near and dear to the black community. The results highlight that black candidates can't ignore issues that concern African Americans or distance themselves from the black community if they hope to maximize their support from the black electorate.

While there certainly are viable alternate explanations for Jackson's higher levels of support in the black community, namely, that Obama ran against Hillary Clinton, who was very popular among black voters, there are also reasons why the results should have been biased toward black voters supporting Obama. While Clinton was the preferred candidate of many black leaders, her negative attacks against Obama along with comments that were perceived as racially tinged should have alienated black voters and led them to be more supportive of her opponent. Also, a bandwagon effect should have increased

Obama's support among black voters. Previous research has shown that voters want to show their public support for the leading candidate in order to better coalesce with societal norms.[22] Along the same lines, black voters may want to say that they supported Michael Dukakis in 1988 in order to prevent perceptions of being less sophisticated voters who supported Jackson because of his race.

The results in chapter 2 indicate that positive racial appeals do not influence white vote choice and increased support among Latinos. In this chapter, however, the results show that whites and Latinos had a strong preference for Barack Obama, the deracialized black candidate. The conflicting results may be tied to Jesse Jackson as a candidate rather than being applicable to all black candidates who utilize positive racial appeals. While Jackson ran a positive racial campaign in 1988, his candidacy was marred by negative and divisive racial rhetoric he had used four years earlier. For example, the press and Jackson's opponents highlighted his use of an anti-Semitic slur and his connection with controversial political figures. As the results in previous chapters show, black candidates who make negative racial appeals perform worse. Jackson may have lost a significant amount of white and Latino support not because of his 1988 campaign but because many white and Latino voters had negative impressions of Jackson from his 1984 campaign.

The results may also be specific to primary voters. White and Latino primary voters may be more approving of black candidates' positive racialized message, but may be hesitant to support Jackson and candidates like him due to concerns about their electability. Jackson's lack of political experience and poor fund-raising performance may have added to these concerns. Moreover, national polls consistently showed that Jackson would lose handily to a number of potential Republican opponents in the general election should he be the nominee.[23] Conversely, Obama performed well in most hypothetical match-ups with Republican opponents in the general election.[24] Jackson's lack of viability may explain why he performed worse than his post-racial counterpart. In the following chapters, I will continue to address these conflicting results by exploring whether positive and/or negative racial appeals are simply associated with a candidate who performs well or worse among voters, such as Jesse Jackson, or if racial appeals can improve or diminish a black candidate's electoral standing.

5

Positive and Negative Racial Appeals in Action

EXPLORING THE INFLUENCE OF RACIAL APPEALS AND
POLITICAL BEHAVIOR OVER TIME

Chapters 3 and 4 demonstrate that when accounting for other factors, black candidates' use of positive and/or negative racial appeals is associated with fluctuating levels of support among voters. However, less is known about whether the use of these racial appeals *changes* these candidates' electoral standing among blacks and other racial/ethnic groups. It is possible that there is something specific to black candidates who use racial appeals that are not being accounted for in the statistical models presented in the previous two chapters. As a result, social scientists, such as myself, may be mistakenly attributing positive and/or negative racialization to the candidates' differing levels of support when some other factor is at play.

For example, black candidates who are lagging by a large margin in the polls and engage in negative racial appeals may be those who are already disliked by the electorate. However, the findings presented in previous chapters — negative racialization is associated with a decline in black candidates' support — could lead us to erroneously conclude that negative racialization decreases a black candidate's voter appeal.[1] To better assess the temporal ordering of racial appeals and related changes in voting behavior, this chapter explores whether the same candidate's level of support fluctuates before and after race is injected into a campaign. In particular, this chapter investigates whether Barack Obama's and Jesse Jackson's levels of support *changed* following two very high-profile events representing positive and negative racial appeals during their campaigns.

The first event, Obama's March 2008 speech on race, "A More Perfect Union," is considered a positive racial appeal. While Obama ran a campaign that was mostly devoid of any discussion about race, the More Perfect Union speech resulted from mounting pressure from both within his campaign and from the media to address the racially divisive remarks of his church's pastor, Reverend Jeremiah A. Wright. Obama's speech exemplified a positive racial appeal. Moreover, given that his speech was carried on every major news outlet, we can assess whether Obama's level of support increased or waned following this appeal, which occurred eight months before the November election.

This chapter also explores whether levels of support for black candidates change after a negative racial appeal. To assess this relationship, I explore the electorate's response to the controversy surrounding Jesse Jackson's use of the term *Hymie,* a racial epithet for Jews, and *Hymietown,* which Jackson used to describe New York City in discussions with reporters during the 1984 Democratic primaries. (Jackson was not aware that he was "on the record" at the time.) Jackson's use of these terms outraged the Jewish community, and he was heavily criticized by the media and political analysts. While not a racial appeal, Jackson's first response to the accusations was to deny he had used these words, as had been first reported by the *Washington Post,* and to argue that his campaign was being unjustly attacked by individuals within the Jewish community and the media for race-based reasons. In other words, Jackson made a negative racial appeal by defending his use of racist terms by saying he was a victim of racism. Thus if negative racial appeals truly decrease the electorate's support for black candidates, we should see Jackson's polled support decline after the Hymietown controversy.

The Wright Controversy and the Growing Significance of Race

Following Super Tuesday, February 5, 2008, Obama won ten primaries and became the frontrunner. Just as it appeared that nothing would stand in his way, on March 13, 2008, ABC News correspondent Brian Ross dropped a bombshell about Obama's pastor, Jeremiah Wright, and controversial statements he had made in his sermons at Trinity United Church of Christ in Chicago. In a 2003 video, Wright chastises the United States for its poor treatment of African Americans: "The government gives them the drugs, builds bigger prisons, passes a three-strike law, and then wants us to sing 'God Bless America.' No, no, no, not God Bless America. God Damn America!" In a another sermon aired on TV, Wright asserted that the government was being influenced by white supremacist groups, and he called the United States the "US of KKK A." Ross noted that "Reverend Wright retired earlier last month, but members of the church say he left a lasting impression on them and Senator Obama."[2] This comment intimated that, if elected president, Obama's policies and behaviors could be shaped by the controversial views of his pastor.

Following the newscast, a number of prominent news stations and newspapers discussed what Reverend Wright meant for Obama's campaign and how much influence he would have on Obama's platform.[3] While Obama in some ways defended Wright by arguing that the clips of his sermons highlight only the negative things that Wright discussed, he also distanced himself from his pastor by saying that he strongly disapproved of the comments presented in the ABC News segment. Obama also mentioned that while he had heard Wright express views that would be considered controversial, he was not in attendance when Wright made the comments presented in the March 13 broadcast.[4]

The issue of race was also injected into the 2008 Democratic primary by former vice presidential candidate Geraldine Ferraro. About a week before the Wright controversy broke, Ferraro argued that Obama's success was partially due to his race. "If Obama was a white man, he would not be in this position. And if he was a woman of any color, he would not be in this position. He happens to be very lucky to be who he is. And the country is caught up in the concept."[5] The Wright and Ferraro statements brought up the issue of race, which had been under the radar during the 2008 election. The growing significance of race gave a number of voters pause about Obama and his ability to win in the general election.[6] With primaries in Pennsylvania, Indiana, and North Carolina still to come and possible defections from super delegates, many called for Obama to address the issue of race head on. Instead of using media interviews or released statements, Obama took a direct approach in his nationally televised More Perfect Union speech on March 18.

The Speech as a Positive Racial Appeal

In this primetime nationally televised speech at Philadelphia's National Constitution Center, Obama addressed the significance of race in American society. The speech embodies a positive racial appeal. Not only did Obama acknowledge racial differences in the United States and the existence of discrimination and racism. He also demonstrated that he was not trying to distance himself from the black community as some of his critics had argued.[7] Instead, he expressed his commitment to advancing the political and social interests of African Americans and underscored his deep bond with the black community.

At one point Obama discussed his common experiences with people who attend black churches across the United States: "Inside the thousands of churches across the city, I imagined the stories of ordinary black people merging with the stories of David and Goliath, Moses and Pharaoh. . . . Those stories—of survival, and freedom, and hope—became our story, my story."[8] Obama showed his critics that although he was raised by a white mother and white grandparents, and he did not descend from slaves, he understood the black community's struggles and perspectives. Moreover, he used terms such as *our* and *my* when referring to the struggles of blacks. In this way, Obama addressed some African Americans' concern that he was distancing himself from them in order to attract white voters.

In contrast to some conservative political pundits who argue that African Americans' poor social standing is due to their lack of effort, Obama also affirmed that he believed that the United States is not yet a post-racial society and that race is a significant barrier to normalcy for African Americans. "As William Faulkner once wrote, 'The past isn't dead and buried. In fact, it isn't even past.' We do not need to recite here the history of racial injustice in this country. But we do need to remind ourselves that so many of the disparities that exist in the African American community today can be directly traced to inequalities passed on from an earlier generation that suffered under the brutal legacy of slavery and Jim Crow." This sentiment is shared by a majority of African Americans, but less so by nonblacks.[9] By stating this openly, Obama refuted arguments that cultural deficiencies in the black community explain continued racial socioeconomic disparities. Moreover, he publically underscored the fact that racism continues to plague the black community in the social, economic, and educational realms.

At other points during Obama's speech, he acknowledged that Reverend Wright's frustrations with the United States were rooted in Wright's experiences with racism. Obama noted that we should not simply disregard Wright as a "kook," but should recognize his attempts to ensure that future generations do not have to endure the same bigotry. Rather than dismissing racial prejudice as a thing of the past, Obama voiced an implicit understanding that a post-racial platform would not be viable and would not improve the position of African Americans. Thus he suggested that his recognition of racial differences could influence some of his policy decisions.

Moreover, Obama noted that more work needed to be done to address racial inequities: "Race is an issue that I believe this nation cannot afford to ignore right now . . . and if we walk away now, if we simply retreat into our respective corners, we will never be able to come together and solve challenges like health care, or education, or the need to find good jobs for every American." While Obama did not offer any specific policy proposals to address racial inequities, he did mention that his campaign would work to improve educational opportunities for all Americans and to increase access to health care. While neither of these issues is race-specific, they are important in the African American community.[10] Obama also said that his campaign would endeavor to further the goals of the civil rights movement in hopes of creating a more racially just society. "But I have asserted a firm conviction—a conviction rooted in my faith in God and my faith in the American people—that working together we can move beyond some of our old racial wounds and that in fact we have no choice if we are to continue on the path of a more perfect union." Obama indeed affirmed that he would work to improve the status of African Americans.

In sum, the More Perfect Union speech had several elements of a positive racial appeal. It highlighted Obama's connection to the black community and his shared frustrations about discrimination. The speech also alluded to Obama's aims of addressing racial differences, should he be elected. Finally, the speech was generally nondivisive—he did not make any specific attacks on individuals. Instead, he discussed racism as an unfortunate fabric of our society, one that all Americans should want to eradicate.

Reaction to the Speech

Obama's "unity" speech received a significant amount of news coverage; most Americans were exposed to the speech in one way or another. Within a day, YouTube reported that the video had been viewed more than a million times.[11] In one Pew poll, over 80 percent of respondents mentioned that they had at least heard something about the speech.[12] Not only was knowledge about the speech pervasive, but it was also well received. According to a CBS News poll, almost 70 percent of viewers thought that Obama did a great job.[13] New Mexico governor Bill Richardson cited this speech in his endorsement of Obama: "Senator Barack Obama addressed the issue of race with the eloquence and sincerity and optimism that we have come to expect of him. He didn't evade the tough issues to soothe us with comforting half-truths; rather, he inspired us by reminding us of the awesome potential residing in our own responsibility."[14] *Mother Jones* reporter David Corn praised Obama on the *PBS NewsHour* for not ignoring the issue of race, which had been increasingly common among politicians. "I thought it was a masterful speech. And I don't think we've seen a politician address these issues so dead-on and do so in a way that wasn't the easy political play." *Chicago Sun-Times* columnist Laura Washington echoed this sentiment: "I think he courageously went far beyond [addressing the Wright controversy] by bringing on the whole issue of race."[15]

Many political observers perceived the speech as demonstrating Obama's connection with the black community. In a discussion on CNN, civil rights activist and Harvard Medical School professor Alvin F. Poussaint noted, "He clearly empathizes with blacks' anger about residual discrimination in America." Roland Martin, a black CNN contributor, said that the speech signified Obama's commitment to addressing racial divisions rather than ignoring them. "W.E.B. Du Bois said the problem in the twentieth century for America is a race problem. What Obama said is we need to make sure the problem of the twenty-first century is not a race problem."[16]

In spite of the outpouring of praise, some political observers criticized Obama for not giving details on how he would bring about these changes. Appearing on the *PBS New Hour*, Earl O. Hutchinson, author of *The Ethnic Presidency: How Race Decides the Race to the White House*, said he would have liked to hear more policy specifics: "You know, Barack, you make great rhetorical speeches. . . . But we really want to know a little bit more to really understand who you are and where you're coming from and what we could expect if you get the nomination and perhaps even win the election. . . . Let's see some initiatives. What can we expect in terms of public policy changes?" In spite of this and similar criticism, most people agreed that Obama endeared himself with the black community in a positive way. However, at the time, whether the public's reaction would yield any electoral support for Obama remained unclear. Moreover, many political analysts suspected that the speech could lead to a backlash from white voters fearing Obama's alliance with the black community.

Jesse Jackson's 1984 Campaign

Jesse Jackson's 1984 campaign started off with low expectations. Jackson had never held elected office, and the field of Democratic contenders included some very experienced politicians, including former vice president Walter Mondale. While many were skeptical of Jackson's ability to succeed, many Americans believed his campaign would benefit black America. One black activist in the Georgia Democratic Party, Holman Edmond Jr., noted, "If you ask me, 'Will he win the presidency or the nomination?' Probably not. But Jackson will win if he simply helps attract enough voters to the polls to help get more local black officials elected."[17] Jackson's chances of winning the nomination were made more difficult by splintered support within the black community. For instance, Detroit mayor Coleman Young and Los Angeles mayor Tom Bradley decided to endorse the primary frontrunner, Mondale, over Jackson partially due to Jackson's low probability of success.

Jackson also had trouble appealing to Jewish voters. Jewish Americans had long been key allies of African Americans during the civil rights movement and were potentially strong allies of Jackson's campaign. Jackson's inability to reach out to this key demographic group was largely due to his support of the Palestinian Liberation Organization (PLO) and his meeting with the organization's leader, Yasser Arafat, in 1979. Moreover, Jackson had argued that the United States should take a more evenhanded approach in the Israeli-Palestinian conflict. As a result, a number of organizations that supported Israel opposed Jackson's candidacy. In spite of these disagreements, Jackson hoped to cobble together enough support from voters of all races/ethnicities to build a viable coalition.

He surprised many with his ability to secure the release of Lt. Robert Goodman, a Navy pilot whose plane had been shot down during a bombing mission over Syrian-controlled Lebanon. While the U.S. State Department had made numerous attempts to bring Goodman back home, all diplomatic efforts failed. Yet an envoy of volunteers led by Jackson successfully secured Goodman's release less than a month before the Iowa caucuses. Jackson received a significant amount of praise from politicians and political pundits; many argued that it made Jackson appear more presidential. A *New York Times* reporter noted, "Republican and Democratic strategists alike seemed startled by Mr. Jackson's skill and audacity as a political gambler. They also agreed that Mr. Jackson's mission had given him additional credibility as a candidate."[18] Jackson also bolstered his candidacy by performing well in early debates with his Democratic rivals.[19] These two factors combined to make him appear to be a viable alternative to Walter Mondale and Colorado U.S. senator Gary Hart. In fact, a New Hampshire primary poll showed that Jackson had tied for second place in this bellwether state. Jackson's projected strong performance in the New Hampshire primary was especially surprising given the state's small number of black voters.[20]

The Hymietown Controversy Derails Jackson's Campaign

While Jackson's candidacy had a series of successes in January and early February 1984, in mid-February Jackson encountered a controversy that made race a salient issue. *Washington Post* reporter Milton Coleman cited an anonymous source who claimed to have heard Jackson using the words *Hymie* for Jews and *Hymietown* to describe New York City to reporters.[21] This story immediately spread, grabbing headlines in every major city and creating a dark cloud over Jackson's campaign. Initially Jackson said that he had no recollection of making such comments.[22] However, this denial did not ease the public's concerns about his candidacy, and it raised serious doubts about his support for the Jewish community. Given the already tumultuous relationship between Jackson and the Jewish electorate, his off-the-cuff comments provided fodder for a number of organizations to mobilize against his candidacy. The increased negative attention had not subsided weeks after the report. Thus Jackson was forced to confront the issue rather than ignore it.

Whereas Obama gave his More Perfect Union speech to address the Wright controversy, Jackson initially took an indirect and combative approach. Instead of admitting he had made the comments and apologizing, he argued that the perpetuation of the controversy was fueled by militant Jewish groups aiming to derail his bid. Jackson stated, "It is clear my campaign is being hounded by certain members of the Jewish community. . . . We're being pursued. We're being persecuted."[23] Jackson later said that a number of Jewish leaders were mounting "an organized effort to destroy [his] campaign."[24] In combination, Jackson's initial reaction to the controversy, first denial and then blame, painted him as a victim. These comments could be perceived as an attempt to rally support by arguing that his campaign was being unfairly attacked. Moreover, like most negative racial appeals, he engaged in divisive racial politics against another ethnic group, Jewish Americans, in an attempt to appeal to his main supporters, black voters.

Jackson's relationship with the Jewish community was further strained by his affiliation with Nation of Islam leader Louis Farrakhan. In the middle of the Hymietown controversy, Jackson joined Farrakhan, a man who had a long and troubled relationship with the Jewish community, at a rally in Chicago. There Farrakhan made remarks that appeared threatening: "If you harm this brother I warn you . . . this will be the last one you harm."[25] Moreover, Farrakhan announced that blacks such as Jesse Jackson were receiving negative press coverage, but that harmful actions by some in the Jewish community were not being covered by the media. "Isn't it interesting that even though you heard all about 'Hymie,' did you know that [Jackson]'s Los Angeles head-quarters was firebombed by members of the Jewish Defense League? Two members of the Jewish Defense League were arrested. Did that get as much publicity?"[26] Farrakhan indicated that Jackson was being unfairly targeted by the media because of racial motivations. This set of divisive appeals may have alienated Jackson from Jewish voters, but sympathy from the black community could have worked to increase Jackson's position. Jackson's affiliation with Farrakhan could be perceived as a racially divisive appeal to black voters.

While the Hymietown comment was not a racial appeal, the reaction of Jackson and his allies—their denial and counter-blame that Jackson was being persecuted and allegedly due to his race—can be categorized as a neg-ative racial appeal. While Jackson apologized within three weeks of the *Washington Post* report and worked hard to repair his relationship with the Jewish community, his initial response is emblematic of a negative racial appeal because it highlighted the unequal treatment he claimed to be receiving from the media and Jewish organizations, and he attributed this treatment to his being black. The appeal was extremely divisive. The Hymietown comment in itself was damaging to Jackson's campaign, but it was his initial response to the controversy—counter-blame and denial—that was most heavily crit-icized. On February 26, *Washington Post* columnist Richard Cohen noted, "Instead of acknowledging that he made an unfortunate remark, and saying that it was a term he heard in his youth and he did not know it was pejorative, Jackson slipped the issue and instead tried to turn the tables on Jews. It was they who were hounding him. It was they who were attacking him. It was they who were harassing him."[27]

The high-profile nature of the comments and coverage of Jackson's response in combination with several surveys that assess his levels of support before and after the controversy enables us to examine how a highly publicized, negative racial appeal can influence black candidates' electoral support among different racial and ethnic groups over time.

Data and Methods

To test whether levels of support of different races and ethnicities changed for Obama after his More Perfect Union speech, I examined state exit polls collected by the national election pool for fifteen primaries and caucuses that occurred after Super Tuesday 2008.[28] These polls were taken in a manner so as to match state demographics and are the same exit polls I used in the analysis of black candidates' electoral support in chapter 4. These data strengthen this analysis because they include a large percentage of voters of various races/ethnicities and their voting decisions.

The dependent variable for these models is whether the respondents voted for Obama in the primary/caucus. I restrict the number of primaries that I examine to between February 6 and June 3, 2008, to ensure that much of the change in support for Obama can be attributed to the speech and is not simply driven by improvements in perceptions of his electability.[29] While some may have been hesitant to support Obama early on because they perceived his White House bid to be overreaching given his lack of experience, following his much-better-than-expected performance on Super Tuesday, many who doubted his ability to win the nomination were converted to support his candidacy. In all, I compare Obama's support in eight states after Super Tuesday but before the More Perfect Union speech and his electoral support in the remaining seven contests after the speech. If positive racial appeals improve an African American candidate's electoral support as we observed in the previous chapters, we should see Obama perform better among different racial/ethnic groups following his speech. This result would demonstrate that changes in preferences for black candidates is dynamic and can be influenced by positive racial appeals.

To test whether negative racial appeals dampen support among voters of various racial/ethnic groups, I examine voters' reactions to the 1984 Hymietown controversy. The comment was reported in the *Washington Post* on February 13, 1984. As described above, the comment quickly drew a polemic response that brought race into the campaign in a divisive manner.

Unfortunately for the purposes of this study, the comment was made before the start of all but one of the 1984 Democratic presidential primaries/

caucuses.[30] However, there are pre-election surveys that include a large enough number of black, Latino, and white respondents to test whether declared support for Jackson declined among these groups after the controversy. In particular, I examine a CBS News survey conducted in January 1984 and a second survey conducted by NBC News at the beginning of March 1984 to determine whether Jackson's support decreased following the Hymietown incident.

The first survey examines political attitudes from a national sample of voting age adults at the beginning of the 1984 presidential primary season (January 14–21, 1984) and was administered by CBS News. The poll includes 1,443 respondents including a sample of over 100 blacks. The survey probes individuals' preferences for the 1984 Democratic presidential nominee through this question: "Eight Democrats have said they are running for president. Who would you like to see the Democrats nominate for president in 1984?" The second poll, the NBC News National Poll, contacted 1,600 adults including about 150 African Americans between March 8 and 10. NBC also asked, "Whom would you most like to see receive the Democratic presidential nomination in 1984?"

If negative racial appeals decrease support for black candidates, we should see a decline in support for Jackson following the Hymietown controversy. However, if negative racial appeals are inconsequential, we should observe no change in support for Jackson.

Results

Table 8A illustrates the average levels of support for Obama in fifteen state exit polls among black, white, and Latino respondents during the 2008 Democratic presidential primaries. Respondents of different races/ethnicities are divided into two groups: the first is the "nontreated" group—respondents before Obama's More Perfect Union speech. The "treated" group includes respondents in states that held primaries after the speech. The descriptive statistics indicate that the speech helped Obama improve his standing in the black community. Before the speech and after Super Tuesday, Obama's levels of black support hovered around 88 percent; however, after the speech, Obama received an average of 92 percent of the black vote in the remaining seven primaries. While the increase in support was only about 4 percent, this indicates that Obama nonetheless significantly improved his standing after making a positive racial appeal. In close elections, this additional support could make an important difference.

The level of white support does not appear to be influenced by Obama's speech or the Wright controversy surrounding it. Obama's level of support in the white community does not vary much. Before the speech, Obama had the

TABLE 8. Support for Obama before and after More Perfect Union speech and support for Jackson before and after Hymietown controversy

A: Obama '08	N	Before race speech/ after Super Tuesday (percent)	N	After race speech (percent)
Black	1,688	87.73	1,675	91.88
White	3,697	40.49	8,970	41.01
Latino	626	36.72	240	53.19
B: Jackson '84	N	Before Hymietown controversy (percent)	N	After Hymietown controversy (percent)
Black	89	39.33	138	18.12
White	872	5.28	1,333	0.98
Latino	46	17.39	40	2.50

Source: A: 2008 exit polls. B: 1984 CBS News National Survey and 2008 NBC News National Survey.

support of 40 percent of white voters, and after the speech he received a statistically insignificant 0.5 percent more support. Thus positive racial appeals can improve a black candidate's level of support among black voters without harming his or her standing too much in the white community.

While only about 37 percent of Latino voters originally supported Obama, their support grew by approximately 16 percent to above 50 percent after the speech. In sum, Obama improved his standing with the electorate and in particular with minority voters. Table 8B displays levels of support for Jesse Jackson from two pre-election surveys for black, white and Latino respondents. As mentioned earlier, the first survey was conducted in January 1984 before the 'Hymietown' controversy and the second was conducted at the beginning of March 1984 immediately following the controversy. The timing of the two polls allows us to assess Jackson's support before and after the 'Hymietown' comment and controversy.

Jackson lost support from all three groups following news reports of his Hymietown remarks. Moreover, the largest decline came from his most stalwart supporters, African Americans. While almost 40 percent of black voters supported Jackson in January 1984, this support decreased by 50 percent in March. Jackson's negative racial appeals damaged his prospects among the voters most likely to be most sympathetic to his campaign.

Latinos also responded negatively to the Hymietown controversy. While about 17 percent of Latinos indicated that Jackson was their first choice in the Democratic primaries in January, fewer than 3 percent supported his candidacy by March. A little more than 5 percent of whites supported Jackson before the Hymietown comment became public. This number dropped to about 1 percent afterwards.

The results presented in table 8B suggest that candidates who engage in divisive, unproductive race-based politics often have a difficult time appealing to any racial/ethnic group. To ensure these results are not artifacts of other factors, including sociodemographic and partisan factors of respondents in polls and surveys before and after the positive and negative racialized appeals analyzed in this chapter, I turn to regression analysis.

Table 9 presents three separate logit regressions predicting support for Obama in the 2008 Democratic presidential primaries/caucuses following Super Tuesday. The regressions are disaggregated by race/ethnicity. The main independent variable of interest is whether the respondent voted for Obama in a caucus/primary election after Obama's March 18, 2008, More Perfect Union speech, denoted in the regression as the treatment variable. The models also include controls for the respondent's age, income, education, gender, partisanship, and region of residence. Moreover, the model controls for the pledged electoral vote difference between Obama and Hillary Clinton prior to the state's primary/caucus.

Black voters appear to be significantly more supportive of Obama following his More Perfect Union speech. In fact, holding all other variables at their mean, black respondents are about 3.5 percent more likely to vote for Obama if their state primary/caucus occurred after his speech. While the magnitude of the effect is small, the results suggest that black candidates' positive racial appeals have a dynamic effect on black electoral support. For African Americans, no other factors increased support for Obama except for gender and Obama's delegate lead. Black women were less supportive of Obama than their male counterparts. This result may be attributed to the fact that Obama's main Democratic primary competitor was a woman, Hillary Rodham Clinton.

As with the findings in the previous chapters, whites do not appear to be too strongly influenced by positive racial appeals. White voters are not significantly more or less likely to support Obama after his More Perfect Union speech. Thus positive racial appeals have an inconsequential impact on white vote choice. Latinos, however, are significantly more supportive of Obama after the speech. Obama's support in the Latino community increases by about 12 percent after the More Perfect Union speech, holding all other variables at their mean. Again, the results suggest that positive racial appeals made by black candidates, such as Obama, can improve black candidates' standing in the growing Latino community.

TABLE 9. Logit regressions predicting support for Obama before and after the More Perfect Union speech

	Black	% change	White	% change	Latino	% change
Treatment (after race speech)	0.38* (0.11)	3.32	−0.02 (0.19)	−0.51	0.47* (0.19)	11.67
Age	−0.01 (0.03)	−0.90	−0.11* (0.02)	21.95	−0.15* (0.03)	29.01
Income	0.02 (0.06)	0.76	0.08* (0.03)	7.57	0.21+ (0.12)	20.02
Education	−0.03 (0.03)	−2.12	0.12* (0.01)	23.24	0.03 (0.03)	5.65
Female	−0.24* (0.10)	−2.14	−0.44* (0.05)	10.77	−0.43* (0.19)	10.61
Democrat	0.24 (0.17)	2.38	−0.61* (0.06)	15.16	−0.34* (0.17)	−8.52
Republican	−0.46 (0.38)	−5.09	−0.15 (0.15)	−3.72	0.01 (0.36)	0.33
Ideology (liberal or conservative)	0.07+ (0.04)	1.38	−0.24* (0.03)	11.95	0.01 (0.05)	0.56
Primary in southern state	−0.04 (0.12)	−0.39	−0.28 (0.20)	−6.88	−0.29 (0.20)	−7.29
Difference in pledged delegate support before primary	−0.00* (0.00)	−4.70	0.00 (0.00)	1.78	0.00 (0.00)	0.35
Constant	2.05* (0.57)		−0.18 (0.34)		0.69 (0.45)	
Observations	3,234		11,835		847	

Source: 2008 Voter News Service exit polls. +Significant at .10, *Significant at .05. Results are derived from three separate logit regressions predicting vote choice for Obama (voted for Obama = 1, did not vote for Obama = 0) for each racial/ethnic group.

Obama's support was strongest among younger Latino and white voters. Obama also performed better with whites with higher levels of income and education. Moreover, both female Latinos and whites were less supportive of Obama than their male counterparts. This perplexing result again is most likely due to the fact that Clinton was the first competitive female presidential candidate. Finally, southern whites tended to be less supportive of Obama. This is not surprising, given the long history of the turbulent black-white relationship in the South.

Table 10 presents results for three separate logit regression models predicting whether a respondent would select Jesse Jackson in the 1984 Democratic presidential primaries in two national pre-election surveys. The treatment variable is of interest as it indicates that respondents were asked about their candidate preference after the Hymietown controversy (i.e., March 1984 survey). The regression model controls for the age, socioeconomic status, partisanship, and gender of the respondent. Moreover, the model includes a control for whether the respondent resided in the South. Table 10 also presents predicted probabilities for the treatment variable derived from the aforementioned models.

The results indicate that the negative racial appeal in the form of the Hymietown controversy decreased Jackson's support among all racial/ethnic groups including African Americans. All else being equal, African Americans were 22 percent less likely to support Jackson after the Hymietown comment than before the controversy, even controlling for other factors such as age, income, and partisanship. White and Latino voters also responded negatively with the same controls. Latinos' electoral support for Jackson declined by a

TABLE 10. Logit regression predicting support for Jackson before and after the Hymietown controversy

	Black	% change	White	% change	Latino	% change
Treatment (after Hymietown)	−1.20* (0.35)	22.43	−1.76* (0.34)	−3.80	−2.01+ (1.19)	11.37
Age	−0.04* (0.01)	34.92	−0.03* (0.01)	−3.24	−0.06 (0.04)	15.95
Income	−0.02 (0.02)	20.28	−0.01 (0.01)	−0.97	−0.01 (0.03)	−2.97
Education	0.14 (0.10)	24.90	0.00 (0.07)	0.01	0.14 (0.21)	8.40
Female	−0.30 (0.36)	−5.39	−0.45 (0.28)	−0.75	−0.64 (0.85)	−3.70
Democrat	0.32 (0.35)	61.74	−0.10 (0.19)	−1.01	0.19 (0.65)	18.46
Republican	−0.19 (0.34)	18.46	0.11 (0.19)	2.51	0.37 (0.67)	57.55
Southerner	0.38 (0.34)	6.78	−0.31 (0.33)	−0.47	0.84 (0.86)	5.66
Constant	−0.56 (1.26)		−1.06 (1.06)		−1.43 (3.32)	
Observations	213		2,053		82	

Source: 1984 CBS National Poll and 1984 NBC National Poll. +Significant at .10, *Significant at .05. Results are derived from three separate logit regressions predicting Jackson as the respondent's preferred candidate (Preferred Jackson = 1, Preferred Jackson = 0) for each racial/ethnic group.

little over 10 percent and whites' electoral support for Jackson declined by about 4 percent after the controversy. The results of the regression model provide additional support for the claim that negative racial appeals damage an African American candidate's electoral support from otherwise sympathetic voters. Moreover, the controversy may explain why Jackson did not achieve the same levels of votes in 1984 as he did in his 1988 presidential primary campaign.

Conclusion

Consistent with the results in previous chapters, the empirical examination of the electorate's responses to Obama's More Perfect Union speech and the Hymietown controversy provide additional support for the claim that positive and negative racial appeals influence electoral support for black candidates. Following Obama's direct and open discussion about race in America, we observed blacks coalescing around his campaign to a greater degree than we saw even after he became the frontrunner following Super Tuesday. Following the speech, Obama's level of support in the black community grew by almost 4 percent. While this increase is small, it does indicate that Obama made marginal gains among black voters through the use of a positive racial appeal. Moreover, it is impressive that Obama was able to improve upon his already extremely strong support in the black community given that there was little room for improvement.

Moreover, Obama's speech also appears to have helped him with the Latino community. Latino presidential candidate Bill Richardson endorsed Obama and cited the speech as a motivating factor. Many others in the Latino community were pleased that Obama did not try to avoid the issue of race in his campaign. The result indicates that by addressing race, Obama was not only reaching out to black voters but was appealing to Latinos as well. This, combined with the results presented in previous chapters, shows that the use of positive racial appeals has a strong potential to increase black candidates' support in minority communities. As the demographic composition of our country changes, today's minority electorate will likely become the majority and thus play an increasingly important role in American politics.

While positive racial appeals improved Obama's standing with minority voters, Jackson's level of support declined precipitously in the heat of the 1984 Hymietown affair. While Jackson had made some headway in the weeks leading up to the New Hampshire primary, the Hymietown controversy ultimately derailed his campaign. He lost about half of the black community's support. Jackson also lost a significant amount of support among whites and Latinos over the same period. While Jackson's ratings rebounded following his apology and attempts to reconcile with the Jewish community, he failed to receive as much support from the black community as he did four years later, in 1988, when he ran a predominately positive racial appeal campaign. One 1984 poll showed that Jackson only had about 50 percent of the black vote.[31] In combination, the results in this chapter again indicate that not all racial appeals are equal. Negative appeals that play on divisive racial/ethnic politics do not yield higher levels of support from black voters. Instead, they often damage black candidates' standing with this electorate. Moreover, the results indicate that it is not just black candidates who are behind in the polls by large margins who tend to use negative racial appeals. Instead, negative racial appeals are in some cases the cause of black candidates' poor electoral performance.

While the results presented in this chapter indicate that attitudes about minority candidates change as a result of positive and negative racial appeals, some may argue that other factors may be at play. For example, as some argue, Obama's uptick in black support following his speech could have been due to the fact that blacks who had doubted his ability to win supported him only after he became the frontrunner. Thus the results could have less to do with Obama's speech on race and more to do with his surging support among pledged delegates to the Democratic National Convention. However, if our comparison group is limited to blacks who voted in state primaries after February 19, before the speech, when he had just won ten straight primaries and was considered the frontrunner, Obama still performed better in the black community after the speech. We also controlled for Obama's delegate lead within the regression models presented earlier. Thus the bandwagon effect alone does not account for the increased support among black voters. The logical explanation for this spike is his speech.

Others may argue that our results could be driven by the fact that Obama expended more resources in the final leg of the primaries. However, a report put out by the Advertising Project of the University of Wisconsin–Madison shows that Obama's campaign spending on advertising was much greater after Super Tuesday and before the More Perfect Union speech than it was in the months after the speech. Moreover, if either of these factors could explain Obama's improved performance in the final months of the primary campaign, then support from all voters, including whites, should have increased after his speech. Given that only minority voter levels of support for Obama increased after the speech provides evidence that his speech in some ways transformed black and Latino support for Obama. While another unspecified factor may have influenced these results, the findings in this chapter in combination with the findings presented in previous chapters, provide additional support for the claim that positive racial appeals can improve a black candidate's standing with the electorate.

While it is difficult to parse out whether Jackson's Hymie comment and/ or response to the comment led to his loss of support among voters of various racial/ethnic groups, the results in this chapter combined with the results presented in chapter 3 provide some evidence that voters are not tolerant of candidates whom they perceive as "playing the race card." While Jackson's apology and subsequent work with the Jewish community allowed him to regain much of the black vote that he had lost due to his inflammatory statements, during the apex of the 1984 controversy, Jackson's response led to a large decline in support among voters of all races/ethnicities. In particular, the controversy hurt Jackson with his base of black voters.

Although black voters want to see black politicians work for their political interests and highlight their connections to the black community, they want this to be done in a productive, positive manner. Thus, regardless of whether Jackson's comment or the response to the comment lowered levels of black support for him, the damage of the controversy considerably diminished Jackson's support from the black community at a critical moment in the 1984 presidential campaign. While voters may not punish candidates for discussing race, many voters will abandon candidates who discuss race in a negative manner.

6

Who Cares?

EXPLORING THE MECHANISMS BEHIND POSITIVE
RACIAL APPEALS AND POLITICAL BEHAVIOR

In the previous chapters, I highlight two main reasons why blacks prefer candidates who make positive racial appeals more than their post-racial counterparts. First, blacks believe racialized black candidates are more likely to advance a racially progressive agenda in office. Second, black voters feel that racialized black candidates are more like them and in turn care about their needs. While the former is based on substantive policy, the latter represents a feeling of mutual understanding between the candidate and the voter. While previous studies thoroughly outline why voters respond negatively to racially divisive appeals,[1] less is known about why individuals, and blacks in particular, would respond to positive racial appeals. Are blacks more supportive of positive racialized black candidates because they believe these candidates will address racial inequities through policy? Do blacks favor black candidates who use positive racial appeals because they feel that these candidates can empathize with them? Or is it a combination of these factors?

One of the surprising findings is that black candidates who make positive racial appeals are not punished by white or Latinos voters. This puzzling result raises the question of why racialized black candidates do not experience a backlash in nonblack electoral support. White and Latino voters may feel differently than black voters about candidates who make positive racial appeals. In particular, if these voters perceive racialized black candidates as favoring the black community over themselves, we should expect non-blacks to be less supportive of their campaigns. However, if racialization has no impact on whites' and Latinos' perceptions of racial favoritism, we gain a better understanding of why black candidates who make positive racial appeals do not alienate these voters.

In this chapter, I further explore why positive racial appeals have a strong effect on some racial/ethnic groups' vote choice but no substantial influence on others. Given that few black candidates make negative racial appeals, and a vast majority make some positive racial appeals, this form of racialization deserves special attention. Moreover, an examination of the mechanism between positive racial appeals and voting behavior has not been studied sufficiently, whereas negative racial appeals' influence on the electorate has been thoroughly analyzed.

To address this shortcoming in the literature, I return to the presidential candidacies of Barack Obama in 2008 and Jesse Jackson in 1988. While twenty years separated the two candidates' bids, the contexts of the elections were similar. The most significant difference between the two candidates was that Jackson made numerous positive racial appeals and Obama took a more deracialized approach (with the one exception of the More Perfect Union speech). By examining how these two high-profile candidates with different campaign styles are perceived in terms of their policy preferences and their ability to sympathize with voters, we gain a better understanding of why positive racial appeals increase black support without alienating white and Latino voters.

Symbols vs. Substance

Black candidates make several symbolic gestures to black voters throughout their campaigns. They reach out, for example, by campaigning with important figures in the black community. Illinois U.S. Senate candidate Carol Moseley Braun campaigned in 1992 with Muhammad Ali and James Earl Jones. Maryland U.S. Senate candidate Michael Steele used hip-hop mogul Russell Simmons in a commercial in 2006. While these appearances by themselves do little to advance black policy interests, they illustrate the black candidate's connections to the black community.[2] These associations may lead black voters to perceive the candidate as racially authentic and as an individual who cares about members of their racial group. When black voters perceive these candidates as sharing their experiences, they may be more enthusiastic and supportive.[3]

Black candidates can also symbolically reach out through their appearances. Previous research shows that appearances make a difference for voters regardless of the campaign content.[4] When 1989 Virginia gubernatorial candidate Douglas Wilder campaigned at a Historically Black College or when 2002 Texas U.S. Senate candidate Ron Kirk campaigned at a Youth Hip-Hop Event, they sent the implicit message to black voters that they would not ignore them. Kirk told potential supporters at the Hip Hop event, "The fact that you have people in office who, even though we may not understand everything that's said on those hip-hop records, at least we know what hip-hop is and at least we're going to answer the phone when you call."[5] Kirk's statement embodies the symbolic message that black candidates send to voters when they make these appearances; they may not always be able to substantively represent black voters, but they have a special connection to the community. Conversely, when candidates do not attend important functions, some will question whether the candidate truly cares about blacks. When Barack Obama decided not to attend the 2008 Black State of the Union, for example, he was criticized by prominent members of the black community, including radio host Tavis Smiley, who insinuated that Obama's absence validated the view that Obama was taking black voters for granted.[6]

In addition to showing empathy for those who share their race, black candidates may improve their standing when they are perceived as advancing blacks' policy preferences. Research shows that a substantial portion of voters make decisions about how to vote based on the candidates' policy platform.[7] Candidates who successfully tie their campaigns to policies that black voters care about may have an easier time getting their support. For example, 1994 Missouri U.S. Senate candidate Alan Wheat, who opposed the death penalty, appealed to black voters because of his potential impact on policy. It is certainly possible that in addition to or in lieu of symbolic racial outreach, black voters are responding to racialized black candidates because they believe they will advance the policy concerns of their community. Black voters' enthusiasm for candidates who make positive racial appeals could be wholly or partially attributed to the substantive policies these candidates support.

White Voters, Latino Voters, and Positive Racial Appeals

A number of studies find black candidates who de-emphasize race in their campaigns are able to attract high levels of support from white voters.[8] Lower levels of support for racialized black candidates may come from fears that these candidates favor members of their own race.[9] White candidates often exploit these potential fears to diminish the support of their black rivals. For example, 2002 Texas U.S. Senate candidate John Cornyn questioned whether his opponent, Ron Kirk, could represent "all" Texans.[10] If racialization increases doubts about policy responsiveness, we should see black candidates who make positive racial appeals receive less support among whites and possibly Latinos.

As with blacks, whites and Latinos may be more supportive of candidates who care about them. In Fenno's classic book *Homestyle: House Members in Their Districts*, he shows that candidates curry favor by immersing themselves in the culture of their districts. This symbolic outreach makes voters feel closer to the candidate regardless of the candidate's race/ethnicity. These gestures may also lead voters to believe that the candidate cares about them. Post-racial black candidates may garner more support from white and Latino voters because they are able to minimize the differences between themselves and members of another race/ethnicity. Conversely, racialized black candidates, such as Jesse Jackson, may lose white and Latino support because they have a more difficult time connecting their experiences with these voters. In sum, white and Latino voters may reject black candidates who do not represent their policy interests and/or fail to show nonblack voters that they can sympathize with them.

Jackson, Obama, and Racialization

In previous chapters, we examine how racialized contexts influence vote choice and an individual's decision to participate in an election. The obvious shortcoming of the work thus far is that it is not known whether whites, blacks, or Latinos perceive racialized candidates to be any different from their post-racial counterparts. To examine whether racialized campaigns influence individuals' perceptions of the candidate's ability to care for them or their racial policy preference, I return to the 1988 presidential campaign of Jesse Jackson and the 2008 presidential campaign of Barack Obama. These campaigns share many similarities. In particular, both occurred in years when Democratic primary voters wanted a more liberal candidate, both candidates faced seasoned opposition, and both endeavored to be the first black president. The campaigns did, however, significantly differ in their message. Jackson ran a campaign that made a number of positive racial appeals, whereas Obama focused almost exclusively on issues that transcend race. Both candidates were very well known, and their candidacies generated a lot of attention. The high-profile nature of these candidates increases the opportunity for voters to know the candidate's platforms.

To determine whether the candidates' racialized message truly influences perceptions of their campaigns, I use the 1988 and 2008 American National Election Study Surveys (ANES). The ANES in both years asks respondents, "Some people feel that government in Washington should make every effort to improve the social and economic position of blacks. Others feel that the government should not make any special effort to help blacks because they should help themselves. Where would you place Jesse Jackson/Barack Obama on this scale?" The scale has been recoded so that scores of 1 indicate that Jackson/Obama believe that blacks should help themselves. Conversely, scores of 7 represent a respondent's belief that Jackson/Obama advocate for government to make special efforts to help blacks. This measure allows us to test whether black, white, and Latino voters differed in their perceptions of the candidates' racial platform. Given Jesse Jackson's racialized campaign, I expect that a higher percentage of respondents will perceive him as more supportive of government taking a proactive role in addressing racial issues.

FIGURE 5. Responses to question "Does Jackson/Obama believe blacks should help themselves (1) or that the government should help blacks (7)," by race

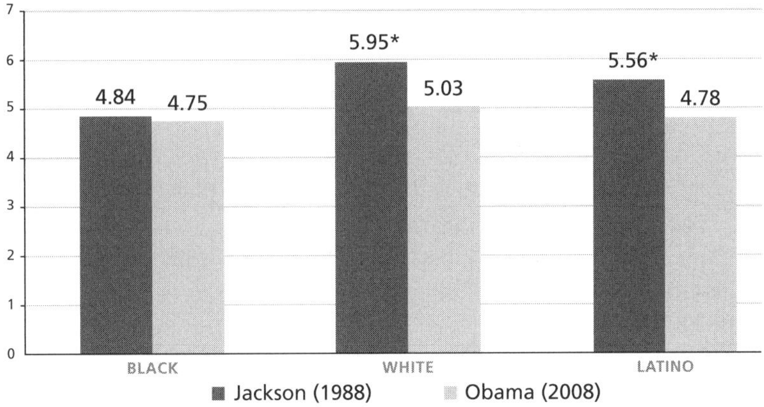

Source: 1988 and 2008 ANES. *Significant at .05. Test of means assesses whether black, white, and Latino respondents had significantly different perceptions of Jackson's and Obama's racial policy preferences. Black N (1988) = 104, black N (2008) = 552, white N (1988) = 1,030, white N (2008) = 664, Latino N (1988) = 32, Latino N (2008) = 459.

In addition to asking about the perceived racial policy preferences of the candidates, the surveys also ask respondents whether they feel the candidates care about them. To assess feelings of concern, the survey asks, "How well does Jesse Jackson/Barack Obama really care about people like you." The scale for this measure ranges from 1 (Not well at all) to 4 (Extremely well). If racialization impacts perceptions of black candidates' ability to empathize with black voters, Jackson should perform better on this measure than Obama among blacks. However, whites and Latinos should feel that Barack Obama, the deracialized candidate, cares more about them.

Results

Figure 5 displays the average score for respondents who are asked whether they believe Jesse Jackson/Barack Obama support policies that increase assistance for blacks on a 7-point scale. The averages are disaggregated by race/ethnicity. The results suggest that racialization does not have a large influence on blacks' perceptions of the candidates' racial agenda. Blacks were slightly more likely to think that Jackson would favor government intervention to improve the position of blacks in the United States more than Obama, but this difference is not statistically significant. In fact, on a 7-point scale, perceptions of Jackson and Obama's interest in promoting government to provide more services to the black community is separated by less than a tenth of a point. The results indicate that blacks are equally likely to see both deracialized and racialized candidates as believing that government should be used to help blacks.

Surprisingly, blacks are less likely than whites and Latinos to believe that Jackson or Obama believe that government should make special efforts to help blacks. This result may be driven by the fact that whites and Latinos are more likely to perceive black candidates as focusing mostly on the black community, whereas blacks are possibly more likely to believe that they will represent them and a broader electorate. Whatever the reason, the results suggest that a racialized campaign does not influence blacks' perceptions of a candidate's platform regarding race and government intervention.

While black voters do perceive the different campaign styles of Jackson and Obama to influence their racial policy preferences, Latinos and whites are statistically more likely to believe that the racialized candidate, Jackson, will favor African Americans. On average, whites gave Jackson a score al-most one point higher on a scale that ranges from 1—Jackson/Obama be-lieve that blacks should help themselves to 7—Jackson/Obama believe that government should help blacks. In fact, whites were the most likely to be-lieve that Jackson would favor the black community. Latinos are also about three-quarters of a point more likely to perceive Jackson as using government to help blacks more than Barack Obama would. In combination, Jackson's significantly lower levels of support from whites and Latinos, as reported in chapter 4, may be due to perceptions that he would provide special favors to the black community. Later in this chapter, I will explore how these results inform us of why Jackson's racialized campaign may have led to a different result than the racialized candidates in chapter 3.[11]

Figure 6 presents the percentage of respondents who feel that Jesse Jack-son/Barack Obama care for them not well at all, not well, well, or extremely well.[12] Blacks overwhelmingly believe that the black presidential candidates care about individuals like themselves. Ninety-five percent of black respon-dents think that Jackson or Obama cares about them well or extremely well. Blacks, however, are much more likely to believe that Jesse Jackson cares for them more than Obama does. While almost three-quarters of blacks felt that Jackson cared about people like them extremely well, only about 60 percent of blacks felt the same way about Obama. This difference is significant at .05 using a chi-square test. Given these results in combination with the null findings displayed in figure 5, the efficacy of positive racial appeals may be tied to the belief that racialized black candidates care more about the black community. While both Obama and Jackson received high levels of black support possibly because blacks perceive these candidates as caring about

FIGURE 6. Responses to question "How well does Jackson/Obama care about people like you," by race

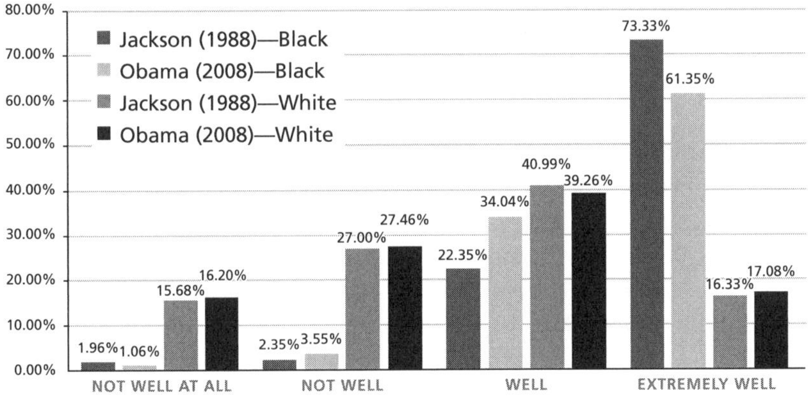

Source: 1988 and 2008 ANES. Black N (1988) = 255, black N (2008) = 282, white N (1988) = 1,537, white N (2008) = 568. Note: Only half of the respondents in the 2008 ANES were asked this question with a traditional four-point score. Chi square score for blacks = 10.65 (DF = 3, sig = .014), chi square score for whites = .5488 (DF = 3, sig = .908), chi square score for Latinos = 1.1655 (DF = 3, sig = .761).

them, those who spend more time working with the black community are perceived as being more empathetic. This difference in perceptions of empathy between racialized candidate Jackson and deracialized candidate Obama may explain why black voters preferred Jackson. In sum, black candidates can improve their standing in the black community if they can demonstrate that they care for individuals who share their race.

While blacks were more likely to believe that Jackson cared about the black community more than Obama did, racial appeals do not appear to have any effect on white or Latino voters' perceptions of empathy. Whites and Latinos (not displayed above) were not significantly more or less likely to believe that Jackson cared about them more than Obama. While they did not see large differences in perceptions of empathy, white Democrats did perceive both candidates as caring about individuals like themselves. Most white and Latino Democratic respondents believe that both Jackson and Obama care about them well or extremely well. Black candidates do not appear to have problems demonstrating to nonblacks that they care about voters who do not share their race/ethnicity. Thus black candidates who use racial appeals like Jackson do not appear to lose support, because they are perceived as not caring about whites or Latinos. Instead, the results in this section in combination with the results presented in figure 5 suggest that some racialized black candidates may lose support from some white and Latino voters because they are perceived as using the government to favor the black community.[13]

Why Is Jesse Different?

The results of the previous analysis provide insight into why blacks respond to positive racial appeals. Rather than being hopeful that black candidates who use these appeals have different racial policy preferences, black candidates benefit from these appeals because they illustrate their connections to the black community. The results of this chapter and the previous chapters still leave the question of why do black candidates who racialize at the state level not lose support from white and Latino voters when Jesse Jackson does? The analysis presented in this and the previous chapter suggests whites' and Latinos' perception of Jesse Jackson favoring blacks may dampen his support. In this section, I provide several explanations for why positive racial appeals by Jesse Jackson may have altered whites' and Latinos' perception of his racial agenda, but may not influence the perceptions of the black candidates analyzed in Chapter 4.

Experience

In Zoltan Hajnel's 2001 and 2007 studies of black candidates and white voters, he finds that whites are wary of black politicians before they have been elected to political office. He attributes this suspicion to whites' fear that black candidates will unfairly favor members of their own community, a concern that blacks generally do not share. After black candidates have experience in office and a legislative record, Hajnal finds that concerns of racial favoritism are abated. Highton (2004) arrives at a similar conclusion in his study of black U.S. House representatives. These studies suggest that when black candidates have a record of legislative action, fears of racial favoritism are assuaged and black incumbents have an easier time drawing support from white voters.

Taken together, Jackson's inability to moderate white and Latino concerns about racial favoritism may be due as much to his rhetoric as it is to his lack of experience. Of the thirty-eight candidates who have campaigned for high-profile statewide office between 1982 and 2010, all but eleven had elected experience. Of the eleven who had no elected experience, about half had some experience in government. Jackson had not served in elected office, and most of his leadership experience was in the civil rights movement. As a result, voters may have been particularly wary of him because of the interaction of the positive racial appeals that he made and the lack of a record to moderate these concerns. The differences in the results in white voter support for Jesse

Jackson and the other high-profile statewide black candidates in the previous chapters could be tied to his lack of experience.

Differences in Positive Racial Appeals

Earlier in this chapter, I argued that black candidates can appeal to the black community through symbolic actions. For example, black candidates who meet with race-based organizations show black voters that they care without necessarily providing substantive policy proposals. Additionally, black candidates can reach out to their base substantively by outlining how their policies advance black politics. The latter type of appeal, however, is probably more likely to increase fears of racial favoritism. Table 11 presents the average positive racialization scores for the top quarter of high-profile statewide black candidates who used positive racial appeals, the bottom quarter of high-profile statewide black candidates who make positive racial appeals, Jesse Jackson, and Barack Obama.[14] Jackson's positive racialization score is at the upper end of the spectrum of all of the high-profile black candidates analyzed in this study. Conversely, Obama is on the other end of this spectrum. Perceptions of Jackson's policy interests may be tied to the fact that he made too many positive racial appeals. Franklin (2010) argues that some black candidates may gain the most traction in the black community without losing white support if they utilize a situational deracialization strategy that combines racial appeals with significant outreach to nonblack voters. Along the same lines, Jesse Borges (1988) and Christian Collet (2008) also argue that minority candidates should use a dual campaign strategy in which they make a number of appeals to minority voters, while still actively focusing on the racial majority. Jackson's predominant focus on racially tinged issues may demonstrate that there is a limit to how many positive racial appeals a candidate can make without being punished.

Moreover, how Jesse Jackson made positive racial appeals differs from the other candidates. According to an analysis that disaggregates positive racial

TABLE 11. Positive racialization scores for black presidential candidates and racialized and nonracialized statewide candidates

Candidate/candidate type	Positive racialization scores
Nonracialized statewide candidates (lower 25%)	0.01
Barack Obama	0.09
Racialized statewide candidates (upper 25%)	0.24
Jesse Jackson	0.29

appeals by policy and symbolic outreach (appearance, language, and associations), 48 percent of Jackson's appeals to black voters came in the form of advocating for racially tinged policies. Conversely, of those in the top third of racialized black candidates, only about 25 percent of positive racialized appeals were based on issues.

Douglas Wilder provides a good example of a racialized candidate who shied away from issue-based appeals. While Wilder scored high on the positive racialization measure, only 20 percent of his positive racial appeals were related to policy. Most of the race-based appeals he made were appearances at black organizations or speeches he gave to predominately black audiences. Given that black voters are responsive to racialization because it increases their belief that the candidate cares, Wilder's approach of symbolically reaching out to blacks garnered significant support from black voters without alienating too many whites and/or Latinos. Jesse Jackson's agenda, which was heavily centered on racialized issues, however, may have led nonblack voters to be worried about how he would govern should he be elected. Thus black candidates should appeal to the black community by focusing on some racial issues, but they must not let racialized issues dominate their agenda.

Conclusion

While previous chapters show that black voters are more supportive of black candidates who make positive racial appeals, less was known about the mechanism that explains this result. The results of this chapter indicate that the use of positive racial appeals does not change blacks' perceptions of black candidates' support for a progressive racial agenda. Instead, the results show that blacks feel that racialized black candidates care more about them. This perception of empathy more than likely explains why black voters in the previous chapters are more supportive of black candidates who appeal to the black community in a positive manner.

The results in this chapter also provide information about why black voters support black candidates at high rates. While both Jackson and Obama received overwhelming support from the black community, blacks were the least likely among all racial/ethnic groups to perceive both candidates as using government to aid blacks. This result indicates that black voters are willing to support black candidates who they perceive to believe that government alone should not be responsible for rectifying the situation of blacks in the United States. This refutes some conservatives' claims that blacks only support co-racial candidates because they will perform special favors for the black community. As a result, statements by former Republican presidential nominee Mitt Romney which suggested that he lost among minority voters because they wanted "gifts" from government are not supported by this analysis.[15] Instead, black voters appear to be more supportive of black candidates because they believe that they will care for individuals like themselves. Moreover, it is these candidates who are perceived as being the least likely to take the black vote for granted. In combination, the results indicate that black voters do not simply want a candidate who will use the government to provide aid to members of the community. Instead, blacks want a co-racial candidate who understands their needs and will work to create opportunities for their community using a multitude of approaches.

Black candidates should not conceal their connections to their racial group by shunning associations with black public figures or missing appearances in front of predominately black audiences. To do so may not help black candidates with white and/or Latino voters, and it might actually diminish their support among blacks who perceive these candidates as lacking empathy for individuals like themselves.

While white and Latino voters are not more or less likely to believe that black candidates who racialize care about them, some black candidates who racialize do increase whites' and Latinos' perceptions that they will use government to provide special favors to blacks. In particular, whites and Latinos believed that Jesse Jackson advocated for the government to provide greater levels of aid to blacks at a significantly higher rate than Obama did. Some white and Latino voters are apprehensive about supporting black candidates who are perceived to favor the black community.[16]

While more research is necessary, by comparing Jesse Jackson with the other black candidates in this project, we learn several lessons about when positive racial appeals influence levels of white support for black candidates. Jesse Jackson, unlike most of the other black candidates in this analysis, did not have elected experience. The differing levels of white support between Jackson and the other candidates suggests that black candidates who use positive racial appeals should have a long paper trail of legislative action to alleviate fears of racial favoritism. Black candidates should also not center their campaign on racial appeals if they want to broaden their electoral support by assuaging concerns of racial favoritism.

Moreover, black candidates should focus more on symbolic appeals to the black community rather than issue-based appeals. Jackson's poor performance among whites and Latinos could be attributed to the fact that his platform was largely made up of issues that would disproportionately benefit African Americans. Other high-profile black candidates appealed to black voters, but did so predominately in a symbolic manner. While black candidates should not shy away from racial issues if they hope to maximize their support in the black community, they should not make these policies a primary part of their campaign platform if they hope to appeal to a broader electorate. Our discussion of Jesse Jackson's campaign in contrast with state-level black candidates provides a better understanding of how black candidates can make positive racial appeals without losing support from nonblack voters. By balancing positive racial appeals with outreach to white and Latino voters, black candidates can maximize their support among blacks without alienating other voters.

Conclusion

A NECESSARY COMPROMISE?

Many expected Artur Davis, a rising star in the Democratic Party, to win the 2010 Democratic nomination for governor of Alabama. Davis was a black politician in the mold of Barack Obama. He was a Harvard Law School graduate and a respected member of the U.S. House of Representatives. Moreover, he took steps to demonstrate his independence from the black community in hopes of appealing to southern conservative white voters. In particular, Davis voted against the Affordable Care Act, criticized revered black congressman Charlie Rangel, and did not seek the endorsements of key black organizations in the state including the Alabama Democratic Conference.

Despite Davis's race-neutral campaign and his large fund-raising advantage, he was defeated in the Democratic primary. To make matters worse, he performed poorly in the African American community. Davis's racially conservative campaign style was cited as one of the reasons he failed to attract black voters. Ellis Cose of *Newsweek* notes, "Davis's biggest mistake . . . was to assume that blacks would rally behind him and that many liberal whites would do the same, making the primary little more than a formality."[1] Instead of replicating the success of Barack Obama in 2008, Artur Davis showed that black candidates who take black votes for granted may be laying the groundwork for their own defeat.

Davis's failed bid for elected office is emblematic of the candidates and campaigns examined in this book. One of the key lessons of this study is that black candidates can't assume black voters will automatically coalesce around their campaigns. Those who work hard to distance themselves from racial issues or black organizations in hopes of appealing to whites run the risk of jeopardizing black support. Moreover, the analysis demonstrates that a deracialized campaign style does not always improve black candidates' standing with white or Latino voters. In fact, some black candidates who make nondivisive racial appeals may actually perform better among some whites and Latinos than their post-racial counterparts. Thus the growing norm of deracialized campaigns could actually be diminishing black candidates' opportunities to succeed at the highest levels of government. Moreover, these campaigns may be fracturing the once unbreakable bond between black voters and black candidates.

In this final chapter, I argue that black voters are very rational and do not automatically support black candidates who do not appeal to their community. I also use the analyses in previous chapters to provide a guide for how black candidates should address race in their campaigns to maximize their opportunities for success. I conclude with a normative discussion about what the racial moderation of black politicians may mean for black political progress should it continue and how a reversal of these trends may improve conditions in the black community.

The Rational Black Voter

I began this book with a quote from actor Samuel L. Jackson in which he argued that he and other likeminded voters made important political decisions based almost purely on race. He even argued that the message of the candidate was inconsequential in his and others' selection of preferred candidates. A growing number of black politicians are implicitly assuming that this argument is correct. Namely, black voters will automatically support their candidacy because of the interaction between their party and their race. Thus it is not surprising to find a growing number of black politicians running deracialized campaigns in hopes of drawing support from white voters without sacrificing black support. However, the results in this study refute the idea that all black voters will automatically support any black candidate. Instead, I find clear evidence that voters are very discerning about which politicians they choose to support.

While many black candidates claim that they will enjoy unwavering support from the black community, the message of the candidate plays an important role in African Americans' electoral decisions. Black voters' ability to understand a candidate's message appears to go beyond just telling black Democrats apart from black Republicans. Black voters are consistently more likely to support candidates who use positive racial appeals in their campaigns than they are to support post-racial black candidates. This finding indicates that not only do black candidates who run deracialized campaigns run the risk of not mobilizing a large segment of the African American community as others have suggested, but they also jeopardize the support of those who do vote.

Moreover, black voters can discern between types of racialization. While racial appeals that provide symbolic or substantive benefits increase black support, the unsubstantial negative injection of race into a political campaign actually harms black candidates' standing with the electorate. Black voters do not simply want a racialized black candidate; they want this candidate to demonstrate their interests in advocating for racial political progress and display empathy for the black community. Similar to the results of Tate (2012) and McIlwain and Caliendo (2011), the results in this book indicate that black voters are turned off by candidates who hope to appeal to the electorate in racially divisive ways.

Overall, many black voters are politically observant and decide who to support based on the potential benefit the candidate will provide should he or she be elected. Black voters don't just want to see someone who looks like them in elected office or someone who discusses race in an unproductive manner; they are most supportive of black politicians who understand the needs and goals of their community. It is these politicians whom blacks most trust to advance their social, political, and economic standing.

The Continuing Significance of Race

In his seminal work on black politics, William Julius Wilson (1980) hypothesized that African Americans will become less of a cohesive voting bloc as blacks' socioeconomic opportunities improved. Wilson argues that as more blacks have the opportunity to advance economically, political and social rifts between the haves and the have-nots in the black community will widen. While black voters still value group cohesion and generally coalesce around the idea of racial equality, a number of studies show that black voters are dividing across a number of cleavages. Andra Gillespie (2012), for example, shows that class divisions within the black community lead wealthier and poorer black voters to support different policies to address racial inequities in the United States. Bositis (2010) provides evidence that younger black voters are less politically efficacious and united than their older counterparts who experienced the civil rights movement. Katherine Tate (2010) demonstrates that black voters are dividing over such issues as school voucher programs, crime policies, and gay marriage.

With this growing diversity in the black community, will black candidates who racialize in a positive manner continue to receive almost unanimous support from black voters? Even though black voters differ in a number of ways, they tend to coalesce around the idea of a united black identity and in support of racial group progress.[2] Table 12 presents public opinion responses for black and white respondents from the 2012 Pew People and the Press Values Survey, which collected information about Americans' attitudes on a wide variety of issues. The table indicates that blacks, even in the age of Obama, have distinct political views about race. Much of this stems from differences in their views about blacks' social standing. According to the Pew

TABLE 12. Differences in blacks' and whites' views about race and government

	Blacks (N = 299)	Whites (N = 2,182)
Views about blacks' social status in the United States		
In the past few years there has been much real improvement in the position of black people in this country	2.22 (.06)***	2.70 (.02)
We have gone too far in pushing equal rights in this country	2.0 (.06)***	2.43 (.02)
Discriminations against blacks are rare today	1.95 (.06)***	2.28 (.02)
Government role in race relations/social welfare		
We should make every possible effort to improve the position of blacks and other minorities, even if it means giving them preferential treatment	2.64 (.09)***	1.96 (.03)
The government should guarantee every citizen has enough to eat and a place to sleep	3.08 (.08)***	2.59 (.03)
The government should help more needy people even if it means going deeper in debt	2.80 (.09)***	2.27 (.03)

Source: 2012 Pew People and the Press Values Survey. Responses range from 1—Completely Disagree, 2—Disagree, 3—Agree, to 4—Completely Agree. ***Significant at .01. Results are derived from a test of means.

survey, blacks were significantly more likely than whites to believe that there has not been enough real improvement for blacks in the past few years, that we as a nation have not gone far enough in pushing for equal rights, that Americans must make every possible effort to improve the position of blacks and other minorities even if it means providing preferential treatment, and that discrimination against blacks is not uncommon. Blacks are also more likely to support government taking an active approach in providing its citizens with a social safety net. Moreover, in the 2012 University of California, Irvine, Outlook on Life and Political Engagement Study survey (which has an oversample of African American respondents) over 60 percent of blacks believed that what happens to blacks in this country has an effect on them.[3] This indicates that even in a so-called post-racial society, blacks still have a strong sense of linked fate with those who share their race.

While blacks may differ in their perceptions of how to improve their standing, black candidates who demonstrate that they care about black voters can garner almost unanimous black support. The research presented in chapter 6 also indicates that black voters do not perceive racial policy differences between racialized and deracialized black candidates. Instead, racialized strategies are effective because they give black voters a sense that the candidate cares about people like them and embraces their connection to the black community. Moreover, black candidates who show their awareness of racial differences implicitly show that they share the unique perspective of other African Americans. Thus it is not surprising to find black voters coalescing around a candidate who may differ from them in certain policy preferences and sometimes partisanship, if this candidate can demonstrate that he or she shares the same goals of racial progress and demonstrates his/her interest in combatting racial inequality. Conversely, black candidates who try to minimize race in their campaigns or ignore the existence of racial differences are perceived as taking the black vote for granted and generally receive less support.

Can Black Candidates Racialize and Still Win?

Political progress for black politicians does not necessarily have to come at the cost of black symbolic or substantive representation. The analysis demonstrates that racialized campaigns are not always a zero-sum venture. Black candidates *can* racialize to appeal to black voters without losing support from whites and Latinos. However, this is dependent on how they racialize. Those who demonstrate symbolically or substantively that their candidacies will address the plights of the black community are the most effective in drawing support from black voters. Moreover, these black candidates in some cases also enjoy higher levels of support from the growing Latino community. However, it is the black candidates who combine some substantive racial appeals with a stronger focus on symbolic racial appeals and have significant political experience who do not sacrifice white voter support.

Symbolic gestures such as speaking at the NAACP or highlighting associations with black leaders allow black candidates to maximize their support from black voters without alienating whites. Candidates who hope to succeed should not make painstaking efforts to disassociate with the black community in hopes that such an approach will increase their support from white voters. An ardent deracialized campaign strategy in which every possible action is taken to distance the candidate from the black community may lead black voters to feel that the candidate does not care about them. It may also appear to blacks that the candidate is taking advantage of the black vote to further their career without offering any symbolic or substantive benefits. Moreover, the deracialized approach may not generate high levels of support from white voters who may perceive these candidates as less genuine. As a result, this campaign strategy is actually counterproductive and may diminish black candidates' opportunities to succeed in majority white settings.

While a majority of white voters still are reluctant to support even popular black candidates,[4] this trend is reversing. Younger white voters show a
greater propensity to support black politicians. As the older generation, who
were socialized during racially turbulent times, becomes a smaller percentage of the population, black candidates may have an easier time garnering
white voter support. Moreover, it may be that younger white voters praise,
rather than punish, black politicians who address racial inequities in their
bids for elected office. This growing acceptance of a positive racialized campaign among white voters combined with the strengthening bond between
black candidates and black voters may improve racialized black politicians'
opportunities for success in the future.

Beyond the world of black and white, the growing Latino population's
preference for racialized black politicians is another reason why black candidates may be better served by addressing black political interests in their
campaign. Given that blacks and Latinos often face the same problems in
the United States, including higher rates of poverty, incarceration, discrimination, and lower levels of income and education, black candidates who
champion issues that concern African Americans could also be inadvertently
or purposely reaching out to Latino voters. Moreover, black candidates who
make appearances and mobilize voters in black neighborhoods are increasingly making contact with Latinos. Given the common space that blacks and
Latinos occupy and their overlapping concerns, the positive racialization
strategy in some cases may not only improve black candidates' standing with
black voters but also help them win the growing Latino vote.

Moreover, the analysis in this study indicates that the purported competition between blacks and Latinos does not preclude these growing minority
groups from coalescing around black candidates. Concerns about candidates
who racialize jeopardizing Latino support because of fears of political competition appear to be unfounded. The common circumstances and obstacles
that blacks and Latinos face in the United States may bind them around
candidates who focus on racial/ethnic disparities rather than deemphasize
them to appeal to white voters. While Jesse Jackson's rainbow coalition failed
in his 1984 and 1988 bids for the White House, a resurgence of this strategy
in the near future may help minority candidates succeed in electoral politics.
As the demographic makeup of our nation changes, black candidates should
reevaluate their strategies to not only focus on white voters but find ways in
which they can appeal to a more diverse electorate.

This is not to say that all forms of racialization are effective. The analysis in
this book consistently demonstrates that black candidates who argue that racism is thwarting their opportunities for success or criticize their opponents

for injecting race into the campaign generally perform worse among voters of all races. Moreover, the relationship between positive racialization and electoral support does not necessarily mean that black candidates should only focus on black voters if they hope to succeed in majority white settings. Black candidates, who focus solely on the black vote, as Al Sharpton did in his 2004 presidential bid, run the risk of being perceived as a "One Trick Pony" with a low likelihood of success. It is certainly possible that white voters' perceptions of racial favoritism from Jesse Jackson in 1988 could be attributed to the fact that many of his campaign appeals were racially tinged. At the state level, where positive racial appeals do not decrease black candidates' white electoral support, the most racialized candidates only made positive racial appeals in about a quarter of the articles that were content coded; even the Racialized Rule Followers did not build their campaigns to solely appeal to black voters.

Instead, most of the Racialized Rule Follower candidates demonstrated the success of Franklin's situational deracialization strategy and Collet's racial toggling strategy. According to Franklin (2010) and Collet (2008), minority candidates can maximize their opportunities for success if they devote some, but not all or even a majority, of their resources to mobilizing and courting co-racial/ethnic voters. At the same time, the minority candidate must also demonstrate his/her ability to transcend race to a general public. The toggling strategy requires minority candidates to demonstrate that they will not take minority voters for granted and to show voters in the racial majority that they will not favor one group over another. The results of this study suggest that some racialization can be a good thing for black candidates. This is especially true if black candidates, like those in the Racialized Rule Followers category, can strike a balance between the tone and quantity of their racial appeals.

The Deracialization Movement and Black Politics

Should black candidates continue to deemphasize race in their campaigns or govern in a way that ignores the black community, we may see the once seemingly unbreakable bond between black candidates and black voters fracture. This has already occurred for several high-profile black candidates. Artur Davis's deracialized strategy led to lackluster support from black voters. Davis is not alone. Washington, D.C., mayor Adrian Fenty suffered defeat in the 2010 District of Columbia mayoral election because of low levels of black electoral support. African Americans in D.C. were frustrated with Fenty's lack of black appointees to important positions in the city. They also felt that Fenty ignored the black community to appease white voters. Even President Barack Obama has his fair share of critics who argue that Obama has not done enough for the black community. Some argue that Obama's lack of effort in mobilizing and appealing to black voters contributed to Democrats' poor performance in the 2010 midterm elections.

The bond between black voters and black candidates is built on the idea that black politicians are in the unique position to understand the plights of the black community and thus care more about those who share their race than white candidates. Like other racial/ethnic groups who have seen their situations improve when they are represented by co-ethnic/co-racial elected officials,[5] blacks too hope that co-racial elected representatives can help end economic, education, and social disparities between themselves and whites.

However, given black elected officials' dismal performances outside of majority-minority districts, few high-profile black candidates have ever been elected. Historically, black voters provided almost unanimous support for black candidates. One reason for this high level of support for even deracialized black candidates such as Barack Obama may be the hope of the unknown. Harris (2012) argued that many black voters were tolerant of Obama's lack of racial appeals in the 2008 and 2012 general election because they were optimistic that he would address racial inequality after each election. As black candidates have the opportunity to break various glass ceilings, black voters may coalesce around black candidates in hopes that he or she will represent their interests once in office. However, as black candidates hold these offices and do little for black voters, we may begin to see a substantial portion of voters demanding more outreach to the black community from their representatives.

If blacks feel that ambitious black elected officials ignore issues that concern their community or take their vote for granted, it would not be surprising to see the post-racial generation of black elected officials continue to lose support in the short term. Spence and McClerking (2010), for example, find that the longer black elected officials held office and did little to change the economic and political fortunes of blacks, the less they empowered their black constituents. In the long term, a deracialized campaign style may lead black voters to be less trusting. As a result, we may see black candidates having a more difficult time mobilizing and energizing black voters without a significant outreach effort.

The destruction of this connection can have catastrophic effects for black political progress. As political scientist Andra Gillespie notes, "We haven't transcended race so much that black politicians don't need every possible black vote. Especially if you harbor higher ambitions."[6] While many have praised post-racial black candidates for their success, in the long term their campaigns may have a deleterious effect on black candidates' hopes of attaining high-profile elected offices. With a large number of white voters still skeptical or unwilling to support black candidates, black candidates' success is often contingent on almost unanimous support from black voters. If this voting bloc stays home or votes for another candidate, we could be entering a period where black gains in elected offices begin to regress.

In addition to increasing descriptive representation, black elected officials and candidates often empower black voters. In cities like Atlanta and Los Angeles, black mayors led black voters to participate more in politics and to have an increased sense of efficacy.[7] However, when blacks feel that the candidates/elected officials do not represent their interest or work to improve conditions in their community, this empowerment effect dissipates. Gilliam and Kauffman (1998), for example, show that black political participation consistently declined the longer Democrat Tom Bradley held the Mayor's Office in Los Angeles. They attribute this decrease in political empowerment to Bradley's unwillingness to take tough positions in defense or in support of blacks Angelinos.

If black candidates and elected officials continue to deemphasize their connection to the black community, levels of black office holding are not the only thing that is threatened. In particular, black voters may become increasingly disillusioned with a political system in which they can't receive both descriptive and substantive representation. As a result, a substantial percentage of black voters may refrain from participating in electoral politics, and the deracialization movement could have a disempowerment effect. If black turnout declines as a result of this disempowerment effect, black candidates may face additional and possibly insurmountable hurdles to attain elected office. Thus this disempowerment effect may lead to a decline in black political representation.

Another possible negative consequence of the deracialized movement may be the marginalization of issues that would address racial inequalities. Recent research demonstrates that black voters are following the lead of deracialized black candidates and are moving ideologically to the center. In contrast to black politicians from the civil rights generation, Tate (2010) argues that black elected officials in recent years are taking fewer liberal stances in order to appeal to a broader electorate. Given that black elected officials, such as Barack Obama, play an integral role in shaping black political attitudes, these centrist stances moderate the black community's political views. This post-racial outlook may be advantageous for groups that hope to incorporate into the political system, but it may not help blacks overcome racial barriers. Harris (2012), for example, argues that the deracialized campaign of Barack Obama has marginalized a number of issues in the black community including higher levels of incarceration and poverty. Supporting a post-racial platform in an era where race is still a problem may lead black voters to dismiss policies that would tangibly improve their opportunities and possibly diminish socioeconomic racial disparities. As a result, black candidates/elected officials who ignore race may make it more difficult for the black community to make political progress in the United States.

However, the deracialized movement does not have to necessarily lead to a decline in black politics. In particular, some black voters' unwillingness to support black candidates who ignore racial issues or who distance themselves from the black community may force candidates to focus more attention on the electorate to avoid being punished at the polls. Harris (2012) argues that the best way for blacks to gain more attention on the national platform is not to provide universal support for black candidates who opt to distance themselves from the black community. He argues that a number of groups such as the LGBT and the religious right have received greater levels of attention by showing lower levels of enthusiasm for candidates who do not do enough to work for their political interests. Following the important elections of Barack Obama, Douglas Wilder, Deval Patrick, and others who broke the "glass ceiling" for black politicians, many black voters may not provide unconditional support to black candidates, as history has already been made. Instead, blacks may become even more discerning about whether their co-racial candidates are going to advance black political interest. If the differences in levels of support for black candidates who utilize positive racial appeals and those who run post-racial campaigns, as were found in chapters 3 and 4, continue to grow, black candidates who want to maximize their support in the black community may be pushed more to focus on their most stalwart supporters.

In turn, this may lead to a virtuous cycle for black politics. If black candidates and elected officials spend more time and resources reaching out to black voters, we may see a more mobilized and hopeful black electorate. This in turn may provide greater incentives for black elected officials in high-profile elected offices to continue to focus more on addressing racial inequalities. In combination, we may see a number of programs being implemented that advance blacks' social and political opportunities. This virtuous cycle between black candidates and the black electorate may lead to a resurgence of black politics rather than what many have argued is its continual decline.

Areas for Future Research

While this book has addressed some important questions about the relationship between black candidates, racial appeals, and voting behavior, many questions still remain. Moreover, this book has raised several questions that should be explored by future studies. In particular, research should assess whether differences exist within the black community with regard to their reactions to positive and negative race-based appeals. Unfortunately, to maximize the number of black and Latino respondents, this study used data sets that contained only basic socio-demographic items. With the right survey instrument, future studies could better explore more nuanced differences within the black community. For example, more research should be done examining whether blacks with higher levels of group consciousness are more supportive of positive and negative racial appeals than those who are less concerned with their racial identity. Given that blacks vary in how important they perceive race to be in their lives, and race-based appeals hinge on voters' concerns with the state of blacks in the United States, we may find that positive and negative racial appeals have different effects on black voters.

Along the same lines, it would be interesting for future studies to examine whether negative racial appeals have any positive influence on segments of the black community. While on average this study shows that blacks punish co-racial candidates for making negative racial appeals, some black voters who believe that discrimination is a large barrier to normalcy for blacks may be sympathetic to this form of outreach. In sum, future research should further explore the differential impact of positive and negative racial appeals within the black community. This examination may be useful for black candidates to further refine their message to different audiences, even among blacks, to expand their electoral opportunities.

While the dearth of Asian Americans in the surveys analyzed in this study precludes any examination of this racial group, future research should examine whether they have different attitudes about positive and negative racial appeals than blacks, Latinos, and whites. While Asian Americans make up a small segment of the electorate now, the growth in immigration from Asia indicates that like Latinos, their electoral significance will continue to grow. Moreover, given that blacks and Asian Americans have shown examples of cooperation and conflict and reside in many of the same cities and states, it would be interesting to examine how Asian Americans respond to racial appeals made by black candidates.

Another area that should be examined is the intersection of gender and race, racial appeals, and voting behavior. Research demonstrates that voters assess male and female African American candidates differently.[8] Moreover, black male and female candidates are perceived as having different strengths and weaknesses. In particular, female black candidates are often perceived as being more liberal than their male counterparts and more interested in addressing problems with discrimination and poverty. As a result, it is possible that voters may judge positive and negative racial appeals made by female candidates as being different than the same appeals made by their male counterparts. While over 90 percent of the statewide candidates that I analyzed in this study were male, the growth of prominent African American female politicians such as California attorney general Kamela Harris, Connecticut state treasurer Denise L. Nappier, and Baltimore mayor Stephanie Rawlings-Blake should increase the number of high-profile black female candidates campaigning in majority white settings. A growth in the number of these female candidates should provide future research with the opportunity to reassess the findings in this study with a more nuanced examination of the intersection of race, gender, and race-based appeals.

Along the same lines, research should examine how the racial hue of the candidate influences the efficacy of positive and negative racial appeals. Previous research has shown that both black and white voters assess lighter and darker skinned candidates differently.[9] In particular, darker skinned candidates generally receive lower levels of support from the electorate. Moreover, the skin tone of an individual shapes views about their racial legitimacy.[10] Given that previous research demonstrates that skin tone matters in how African Americans are perceived, it is also possible that black candidates of different skin tone may be judged differently for engaging race-based appeals as well. Thus future studies should examine how the complexion of the candidate interacts with the use of positive and negative racial appeals to influence the electorate. Such a study would be best suited for experiments in a controlled environment where the candidates' skin tone could be carefully manipulated.

While the goal of this book was to explore the differences between positive and negative racial appeals, a more nuanced study should explore whether black candidates either improve or diminish their standing with the electorate by making only positive *implicit* racial appeals, positive *explicit* racial appeals, or a combination in their campaigns. The work done in this book offers some clues to such research. The analysis of Obama's More Perfect Union speech suggests that positive explicit racial appeals have the power to improve black candidates' standing in the community without sacrificing support from other racial/ethnic groups. I also find in a separate analysis not reported in this book that the percent of explicit positive racial appeals made by black candidates at the state level increases their support among both blacks and Latinos. Moreover, this analysis shows that the more black candidates engage in implicit positive racial appeals, the higher their levels of support from black voters.

Still more needs to be done to understand the strengths and weaknesses of positive implicit and explicit racial appeals. In particular, future research should endeavor to better isolate the influence of these distinct forms of positive racial appeals on the electorate. The analysis done in this study utilizes black candidates who generally engage in both forms of positive racial appeals if they discuss race at all. Thus it is difficult to disaggregate the effects of positive implicit and explicit racial appeals on voting behavior. Moreover, future research should further probe whether voters perceive positive implicit or explicit racial appeals as distinct forms of outreach. Given that the work in this study seems to indicate that positive implicit and explicit appeals have a similar effect, it is possible that even implicit positive racial appeals are perceived as being overt when they come from an African American candidate.

Finally, one of the perplexing findings in this study is that racial appeals did not have a large influence on black turnout. While this non-result was consistent across the state and national levels, it is possible that the self-reported nature of voting in both the Current Population Survey and the American National Election Study may be influencing the results. More work should be done assessing this relationship using vote-validated data. However, given the consistency of the results across levels and the fact that the same surveys are used in the comparisons, it is less likely that the overreporting of voting alone can be attributed to this result. Nonetheless, future studies should reassess the findings in chapters 2 and 4 using vote-validated data.

Conclusion

Following the success of a number of deracialized black candidates in the 1989 elections, including New York City mayor David Dinkins and Virginia governor L. Douglas Wilder, there were a number of scholars and political pundits who argued that black candidates will have to run deracialized campaigns if they have any hope of succeeding in majority white contexts. At the same time there were fears that the deracialized campaign styles of these candidates would force blacks to sacrifice their substantive political interests to see someone like themselves in the most prestigious government offices. In Robert Smith's 1990 article, "Recent Elections and Black Politics: The Maturation or Death of Black Politics?" he argues that if blacks continue to deemphasize race in their campaigns, "the new black politician will just be a shell of himself" (161). Smith concludes by arguing, "The elections of 1989 represent . . . not a maturation of black politics, but still further evidence of its continued degeneration (161). The de-emphasis of black candidates' connection to the black community was a necessary compromise that black politicians would have to make if they hoped to succeed in electoral politics, but it meant that black politicians would not be able to address blacks' most pressing concerns.

Despite the fear of a degeneration of black politics, a number of scholars and political pundits warn that while black candidates may deemphasize race in their campaigns, this does not mean that the black community will automatically support them. McCormick and Jones (1993), in their study of deracialization, caution black candidates not to take an overtly deracialized approach as it may lead to lower levels of black support. The authors suggest that the deracialization style has its limits and may not always be the most effective campaign strategy.

In recent years, predictions about the limits of the deracialized campaign styles are borne out in anecdotal examples and in social science research. More than twenty years after the success of a number of deracialized black candidates in the 1989 elections, blacks still remain largely underrepresented in majority-white settings. Thus, in spite of more than two decades of deracialized black candidates, black politicians have yet to make dramatic inroads into elected office among majority-white electorates. Moreover, in a 2012 *New Yorker* article, "The End of the New Black Politician," William Jelani Cobb details how the once infallible deracialization campaign strategy may no longer be the only path to electoral success. Cobb argues that black politicians, like Newark mayor Cory Booker, Alabama congressman Artur Davis, and Washington mayor Adrian Fenty, who govern or campaign in ways that deemphasize their connections to the black community, often face an electoral backlash.

The findings in this book corroborate Cobb's claims through a systematic analysis of a large number of cases. This study provides an alternate prescription for how black candidates should address race in their campaigns. When controlling for a number of factors, black candidates who at least make some attempts to appeal to black voters perform better than their counterparts who ignore race. This goes counter to the suggestions of many practitioners and scholars who argue that black candidates can only succeed if they minimize their connections to other African Americans. While this was troubling to several black political leaders, many saw it as a necessary compromise for success. The research in this book suggests that, if the conditions are right, black candidates can reach the highest echelons of American politics without sacrificing their presumed ties to the black community. Moreover, it indicates that black political advancement does not necessarily have to mean the death of black politics.

Appendix

Chapter 2

Content Coding for Opponent Racialization and Media Racialization

RACIST APPEALS BY THE OPPONENT

In addition to black candidates using racial appeals, it is not uncommon for their white opponents to also make race a salient issue in biracial elections. Unfortunately, these racial appeals often come in the form of negative stereotypes of black candidates and are used to appeal to anti-minority factions (see McIlwain and Caliendo 2011 for a good discussion of racial vs. racist appeals). Opponents are given scores of 0 if they either discussed their strengths or highlighted their opponent's weaknesses with issues that are not associated with race. These issues are also associated with scores of 0 for black candidates presented in table 1. For example, if white candidates attacked their opponent for being weak on the environment, then they were not injecting race into the election, just negativity, and are given a score of 0. If white candidates in a biracial election attacked their opponent on issues that are implicitly tied to race (the same issues listed for black candidates with a score of 1 in table 1), they are given a score of 1 on the implicit racist appeals. For example, when Kerry Healey campaigned against black candidate Deval Patrick for governor of Massachusetts in 2006, she attacked Patrick for being too lenient on crime. While the appeals were not explicitly racist, they may have conjured up fears that blacks do not take crime seriously.

When white candidates attack their opponent on issues that are explicitly about race such as affirmative action and/or civil rights legislation, they are given a score of 1 on the explicit racial appeal measure. The most infamous example of this would be Jesse Helms's "Hands" ad, which showed a white hand crumpling up a rejection letter, while the narrator says, "You needed that job, and you were the best qualified, but they had to give it to a minority because of a racial quota. Is that really fair? Harvey Gantt says it is." Such an advertisement explicitly attacks a black candidate on issues regarding race. Moreover, it creates a racially hostile environment.

TABLE 13. Number of current population survey respondents by election

Candidate	Year	Black	White	Latino
Tom Bradley	1982	38	683	47
Tom Bradley	1986	491	5,124	687
William Lucas	1986	502	3,559	—
Maurice Dawkins	1988	152	989	—
Harvey Gantt	1990	42	1,627	87
Theo Mitchell	1990	12	462	20
Carol Moseley Braun	1992	437	2,949	364
Alan Keyes	1992	177	705	70
Ron Sims	1994	20	966	13
Alan Wheat	1994	84	832	3
Harvey Gantt	1996	345	1,699	20
Gary Franks	1998	39	713	—
Carol Moseley Braun	1998	403	2,477	149
Jack E. Robinson	2000	86	1,539	69
Joe Neal	2002	94	1,326	190
Carl McCall	2002	523	3,215	375
Ron Kirk	2002	401	2,067	826
Denise Majette	2004	516	1,016	20
Marvin Scott	2004	108	1,503	40
Ken Blackwell	2006	218	2,179	52
Erik Fleming	2006	274	512	14
Deval Patrick	2006	34	1,158	51
Michael Steele	2006	474	1,372	65
Harold Ford Jr.	2006	110	1,045	10
Lynn Swann	2006	154	2,443	76
Michael Thurmond	2010	438	1,027	49
Kendrick Meek	2010	334	1,953	497
Alvin Greene	2010	328	816	15
Deval Patrick	2010	60	1,047	83

White candidates are also scored based on whether or not they used racially coded language. As with black candidates, the audience matters. White candidates who use *us, we,* or *them* in a context where blacks and whites have an equal probability of being in the audience are given a score of 0. White candidates who use the same language in a setting where white voters are likely a large segment of the audience, such as at a Republican convention or in cities such as Springfield, Missouri, which is overwhelmingly white, are given a score of 1 on

TABLE 14. Positive and negative racial appeals and voter turnout by racial/ethnic groups

Candidate	Positive racial appeal	Negative racial appeal	% black turnout	% white turnout	% Latino turnout
Tom Bradley (D) 1982	0.02	0.02	68.42	61.35	70.21
Tom Bradley (D) 1986	0.04	0.00	52.75	59.89	39.59
William Lucas (R) 1986	0.15	0.02	52.79	47.23	—
Maurice Dawkins (R) 1988	0.31	0.13	45.39	59.86	—
Harvey Gantt (D) 1990	0.04	0.05	47.62	40.32	34.48
Theo Mitchell (D) 1990	0.17	0.29	33.33	40.48	40.00
Carol Moseley Braun (D) 1992	0.08	0.00	75.06	75.75	50.27
Alan Keyes (R) 1992	0.24	0.17	67.23	73.90	55.71
Ron Sims (D) 1994	0.02	0.00	30.00	54.45	53.85
Alan Wheat (D) 1994	0.09	0.00	47.62	62.26	0.00
Harvey Gantt (D) 1996	0.11	0.00	57.97	62.68	20.00
Carol Moseley Braun (D) 1998	0.05	0.01	65.76	52.24	44.30
Gary Franks (R) 1998	0.10	0.00	51.28	55.40	—
Jack Robinson (R) 2000	0.00	0.03	66.28	74.59	28.99
Joseph Neal (D) 2002	0.02	0.00	43.62	53.32	26.84
Carl McCall (D) 2002	0.11	0.00	50.67	53.75	34.40
Ron Kirk (D) 2002	0.32	0.05	54.36	52.25	32.20
Denise Majette (D) 2004	0.03	0.00	69.77	65.65	40.00
Marvin Scott (R) 2004	0.04	0.00	67.59	67.20	40.00
Kenneth Blackwell (R) 2006	0.09	0.00	53.67	61.73	36.54
Erik Fleming (D) 2006	0.29	0.02	57.66	45.12	0.00
Deval Patrick (D) 2006	0.03	0.05	52.94	64.51	37.25
Michael Steele (R) 2006	0.27	0.00	62.03	64.21	63.08
Harold Ford (D) 2006	0.10	0.00	54.55	53.97	20.00
Lynn Swann (R) 2006	0.09	0.00	56.49	55.18	31.58
Michael Thurmond (D) 2010	0.01	0.00	57.53	54.53	30.61
Kendrick Meek (D) 2010	0.03	0.00	56.89	59.45	49.09
Alvin Greene (D) 2010	0.00	0.00	62.20	56.99	13.33
Deval Patrick (D) 2010	0.03	0.00	51.67	68.48	20.48

the implicit racist appeal measure. As with black candidates, it can be assumed that the appeal was made to white voters, but it is not explicit because the racial composition of the audience is unknown. Candidates who used racially coded language in reference to race are given a score of 1 on the explicit racial appeal measure. For example, during the 2002 Texas U.S. Senate campaign, a reporter

TABLE 15. Logit regression predicting voting for blacks, whites, and Latinos (full model)

	A: Blacks	% change	B: Whites	% change	C: Latinos	% change
Black candidate positive racialization	0.46 (0.53)	4	0.28 (0.39)	2	1.20*** (0.38)	9
Black candidate negative racialization	−2.80 (2.03)	−20	−1.95*** (0.75)	−14	−1.29 (1.55)	−8
White candidate positive racialization	4.27* (2.56)	15	1.09 (1.10)	4	7.01*** (1.32)	27
White candidate negative racialization	−2.91*** (1.03)	−38	−0.24 (0.75)	−3	−3.60* (2.07)	−36
Media racialization	0.10 (0.15)	2	−0.49*** (0.14)	−13	1.08 (0.77)	25
Democrat (candidate)	0.15 (0.17)	4	0.01 (0.08)	0	0.14 (0.13)	3
Experience (proportional to opponent)	0.00 (0.00)	0	−0.00 (0.00)	−3	−0.00** (0.00)	−18
Spending (proportional to opponent)	0.34** (0.13)	25	0.06 (0.09)	5	0.32 (0.22)	28
Non-incumbent candidate	−0.12 (0.12)	−3	−0.14* (0.08)	−3	−0.33*** (0.11)	−8
Democratic state	−0.73** (0.37)	−10	−0.68*** (0.15)	−10	0.89*** (0.26)	12
Campaigning for governor	−0.06 (0.19)	−1	0.17 (0.12)	4	0.04 (0.20)	1
1980–89	−0.25 (0.19)	−6	0.04 (0.12)	1	−0.60*** (0.20)	−14
1990–99	0.45*** (0.16)	10	0.08 (0.09)	2	0.43*** (0.13)	10
Campaign in southern state	−0.04 (0.17)	−1	−0.02 (0.12)	0	0.01 (0.17)	0
Percentage of articles mentioning candidate only once	0.36 (0.72)	4	−0.02 (0.55)	0	0.36 (1.27)	4
Female (respondent)	0.24*** (0.04)	6	0.04 (0.02)	1	−0.05 (0.10)	−1
Age (respondent)	0.04*** (0.00)	58	0.04*** (0.00)	62	0.05*** (0.00)	69
Income (respondent)	0.36*** (0.05)	34	0.30*** (0.02)	30	0.16*** (0.05)	16
Education (respondent)	0.17*** (0.01)	68	0.23*** (0.01)	79	0.14*** (0.01)	53

(continued)

TABLE 15 (*continued*)

	A: Blacks	% change	B: Whites	% change	C: Latinos	% change
Average year turnout	3.85*** (1.00)	19	2.17** (1.00)	11	0.91 (1.58)	5
Average state turnout	−0.47 (1.05)	−4	2.91*** (0.94)	22	3.06** (1.27)	23
Constant	−2.27* (1.31)		−6.11*** (1.04)		−3.09* (1.86)	
Observations	6,218		42,442		3,575	
Clusters	29		29		26	

Source: 1982–2010 Current Population Survey. * Significant at .10, ** Significant at .05 *** Significant at .01. Robust standard errors in parentheses. The standard errors are clustered for 26–29 unique elections. "Respondent" indicates that these are respondent level attributes rather than attributes of the candidate.

from the *Austin American Statesman* noted, "John Cornyn said he would be a senator for 'all Texans' and pointed to his efforts against the use of race in determining whether convicted murderers should be sentenced to death." The reference of "all Texans" implies that his opponent, Ron Kirk, would only represent African Americans. The connection of the racially coded language to a policy regarding race makes this appeal explicitly racial. White candidates are also given a score of 1 on the explicit racist appeal measure if they used racially coded language in a context in which the newspaper describes the audience as being overwhelmingly white. Finally, white candidates are given a score of 1 on the explicit racial appeal measure if they used racially coded language in an advertisement. Similar to positive racial appeals for black candidates, the opponent's negative racial appeal is a factor score of both implicit and explicit racist appeals.

MEDIA RACIALIZATION

Bryan D'Andra Orey (1996) finds that black and white candidates are not the only political actors who have the ability to make race an issue in a campaign. Instead, he finds that even when black candidates and their opponents abstain from racial discussions, the media often highlights the race of the candidate. Reeves (1997) and McIlwain and Caliendo (2011) arrive at similar conclusions in their examinations of black candidates in biracial elections. To account for the media's injection of race into an election the models presented in chapters 2 and 3 also account for racial coverage by newspapers. The media's injection of race is scored on a three-point scale.

When the media does not mention the race of the candidates in the article, the media is given a score of 0 on the measure. If the media mentions the race of the candidates in the article briefly or in passing, then the media is given a score of 1. For example, when the media mentions that a candidate will be the first African American elected to the Governor's Office or to the U.S. Senate in the state, the article is given a score of 1. When Harold Ford Jr. campaigned for the U.S. Senate in Tennessee, it was not uncommon for newspapers to mention that he would be the first black senator from the South since Reconstruction. Another example of the media mentioning the candidate's race in passing is when Michael Steele campaigned for the U.S. Senate in Maryland and a number of articles noted that Steele is a "black Republican." While these articles highlight the race of the candidate, this use of race is tangential to their coverage of the campaign.

Articles that make race a focal part of the coverage, rather than mentioning the race of the candidate in passing, are given a score of 2. In particular, if more than a quarter of the article is devoted to the candidate's race or if the candidate's race is highlighted in the headline, then the article is given a score of 2. For example, A *Washington Post* article about the 1982 California gubernatorial election was titled "The Race Issue in the California Campaign." The coverage in this article highlighted Bradley's historic bid to be the first African American governor and investigated what this momentous achievement meant to black voters. The overt racial frame of the article made race a salient issue in the campaign and thus was given a score of 2 for the media racialization measure.

Chapter 3

TABLE 16. Polling organization and respondents for each election

Candidate	Year	Polling organization	Black	White	Latino
Tom Bradley	1982	CBS News	237	2,553	152
Tom Bradley	1986	CBS News	362	1,898	141
Maurice Dawkins	1988	CBS News	49	286	2
Douglas Wilder	1989	CBS News/New York Times	213	911	15
Harvey Gantt	1990	Voter Research & Surveys	505	1,656	5
Theo Mitchell	1990	Voter Research & Surveys	421	1,383	4
Carol Moseley Braun	1992	Voter Research & Surveys	224	1,296	35
Alan Keyes	1992	Voter Research & Surveys	165	511	5
Ron Sims	1994	Voter News Service	56	1,276	24
Alan Wheat	1994	Voter News Service	199	969	11

(continued)

TABLE 16 (*continued*)

Candidate	Year	Polling organization	Black	White	Latino
Harvey Gantt	1996	Voter News Service	574	1,544	9
Gary Franks	1998	Voter News Service	82	1,268	41
Carol Moseley Braun	1998	Voter News Service	274	1,271	32
Jack E. Robinson	2000	Voter News Service	37	593	21
Carl McCall	2002	Voter News Service	22	996	33
Ron Kirk	2002	Voter News Service	241	1,104	214
Denise Majette	2004	Edison Media Research/ Mitofsky International	389	1,095	63
Marvin Scott	2004	Edison Media Research/ Mitofsky International	57	806	32
Ken Blackwell	2006	Edison Media Research/ Mitofsky International	308	2,105	24
Deval Patrick	2006	Edison Media Research/ Mitofsky International	61	520	36
Michael Steele	2006	Edison Media Research/ Mitofsky International	414	1,168	25
Harold Ford Jr.	2006	Edison Media Research/ Mitofsky International	312	2,109	24
Lynn Swann	2006	Edison Media Research/ Mitofsky International	324	1,990	40
Erik Fleming	2008	Edison Media Research/ Mitofsky International	379	576	36
Vivian Figures	2008	Edison Media Research/ Mitofsky International	377	607	43
Kendrick Meek	2010	Edison Research	524	2,216	327
Alvin Greene	2010	Edison Research	530	1,225	46

TABLE 17. Positive and negative racial appeals and electoral support among different racial/ethnic groups

Candidate	Positive racial appeal	Negative racial appeal	% black support	% white support	% Latino support
Tom Bradley (D) 1982	0.02	0.02	89.03	43.24	67.76
Tom Bradley (D) 1986	0.04	0	89.23	34.67	62.41
Maurice Dawkins (R) 1998	0.31	0.13	26.53	31.82	98.00
Douglas Wilder (D) 1989	0.17	0	92.02	43.80	60.00
Harvey Gantt (D) 1990	0.04	0.05	95.25	38.59	60.00
Theo Mitchell (D) 1990	0.17	0.29	82.90	10.41	25.00

(*continued*)

TABLE 17 (*continued*)

Candidate	Positive racial appeal	Negative racial appeal	% black support	% white support	% Latino support
Carol Moseley Braun (D) 1992	0.08	0	95.54	53.01	71.43
Alan Keyes (R) 1992	0.24	0.17	9.09	30.92	40.00
Ron Sims (D) 1994	0.02	0	80.36	43.50	54.17
Alan Wheat (D) 1994	0.09	0	90.95	34.47	45.45
Harvey Gantt (D) 1996	0.11	0	91.29	38.54	55.56
Gary Franks (R) 1998	0.10	0	26.83	33.44	7.32
Carol Moseley Braun (D) 1998	0.05	0.01	93.43	38.39	46.88
Jack Robinson (R) 2000	0.00	0.03	2.70	11.97	14.29
Carl McCall (D) 2002	0.11	0	72.73	22.99	36.36
Ron Kirk (D) 2002	0.32	0.05	94.19	31.43	67.76
Denise Majette (D) 2004	0.03	0	87.15	23.11	41.27
Marvin Scott (R) 2004	0.04	0	8.77	42.93	12.50
Kenneth Blackwell (R) 2006	0.09	0	3.25	35.11	29.17
Deval Patrick (D) 2006	0.03	0.05	93.44	64.62	80.56
Michael Steele (R) 2006	0.27	0	23.43	47.95	36.00
Harold Ford (D) 2006	0.10	0	95.51	41.54	58.33
Lynn Swann (R) 2006	0.09	0	8.02	38.84	10.00
Vivian Figures (D) 2008	0.00	0	84.88	16.47	53.49
Erik Fleming (D) 2008	0.02	0.02	89.45	7.81	69.44
Kendrick Meek (D) 2010	0.03	0	77.10	12.77	28.75
Alvin Greene (D) 2010	0.00	0	68.87	8.08	43.48

TABLE 18. Logit regression predicting support for black candidates among blacks, whites, and Latinos (full model)

	A: Blacks	% change	B: Whites	% change	C: Latinos	% change
Black candidate, positive racialization	7.96*** (2.61)	29	2.06 (1.93)	15	2.23* (1.35)	18
Black candidate, negative racialization	−6.45*** (1.96)	−40.00	−5.27*** (1.83)	−24	4.54 (4.14)	31
White candidate, positive racialization	1.00 (1.53)	8	0.31 (1.38)	4	7.33** (2.98)	68
White candidate, negative racialization	−1.67 (2.86)	−4	3.36 (2.32)	12	7.01* (4.05)	26

(*continued*)

TABLE 18 (*continued*)

	A: Blacks	% change	B: Whites	% change	C: Latinos	% change
Media racialization	0.42 (0.62)	6	0.96** (0.41)	20	−2.15* (1.16)	−44
Democrat (candidate)	3.79*** (0.42)	73	0.1 (0.23)	2	0.80** (0.32)	19
Experience (proportional to opponent)	0.01 (0.01)	8	0.01 (0.01)	4	0.01 (0.01)	−2
Spend (proportional to opponent)	0.02 (0.27)	1	0.08 (0.19)	6	−0.72* (0.43)	−49
Non-incumbent candidate	−0.12 (0.33)	−2	−0.01 (0.25)	0	−0.12 (0.37)	−3
Democratic support (state)	0.09 (1.27)	1	1.77* (1.01)	22	−0.99 (1.52)	−15
Campaign in southern state	−0.41 (0.28)	−6	−0.1 (0.17)	−2	−0.43 (0.45)	−11
Age (respondent)	−0.01*** (0.00)	−11	−0.01*** (0.00)	−9	0 (0.01)	−6
Female (respondent)	0.04 (0.09)	1	0.09* (0.05)	2	−0.06 (0.10)	−2
Income (respondent)	0.02 (0.03)	2	−0.02 (0.02)	−2	0.01 (0.05)	2
Same party as candidate (respondent)	1.82*** (0.18)	32	2.34*** (0.11)	51	2.19*** (0.19)	50
Percentage of articles mentioning candidate only once	0.74 (1.31)	5	−2.25*** (0.85)	−21	−2.28 (1.89)	−25
1980–89	−1.02*** (0.24)	−12	0.21 (0.23)	4	0.38 (0.56)	9
1990–99	0.01 (0.31)	0.10	0.66*** (0.23)	14	−0.15 (0.38)	4
Campaigning for governor	−0.2 (0.17)	−3	−0.16 (0.14)	−3	−0.36 (0.24)	9
Constant	−3.52** (1.59)		−3.09** (1.21)		−6.99*** (2.46)	
Observations	6,052		29,146		1,144	
Clusters	27		27		27	

+Significant at .10, *Significant at .10, **Significant at .05, ***Significant at .01. Results are derived from three separate logit regressions predicting vote choice (voted for a black candidate = 1, did not vote for a black candidate = 0) for each racial/ethnic group. "Respondent" indicates that these are respondent level attributes rather than attributes of the candidate.

Chapter 4

TABLE 19. Predicted probabilities from logit regression predicting turnout in the 1988 and 2008 Democratic presidential primaries for Democrats alone

Voter turnout	Black	% change	White	% change
Jackson (1988)	0.46	11	−0.70***	−17
	(0.40)		(0.22)	
Age	0.03***	52	0.03***	60
	(0.01)		(0,01)	
Income	0.22*	23	0.19*	19
	(0.14)		(0.10)	
Education	0.26***	72	0.27***	62
	(0.06)		(0.04)	
Female	0.31	8	−0.04	−1
	(0.24)		(0.17)	
Southerner	−0.25	−6	0.76***	19
	(0.42)		(0.25)	
Delegate surplus/deficit	0.00	−13	0.001***	35
	(0.00)		0.00	
Constant	−4.93***		−5.14***	
	(1.00)		(0.67)	
Observations	361		726	

* Significant at .10, ***Significant at .01. Results are derived from two separate logit regressions predicting voter turnout (voted in primary election=1, did not vote in primary election=0) for each racial/ethnic group.

TABLE 20. Predicted probabilities from logit regression predicting electoral support for Jesse Jackson '88 and Barack Obama '08

DV = Support for black candidate	Black	% change	White	% change	Latino	% change
Jackson (1988)	1.14***	9	−1.91***	−32	−0.33**	−8
	(0.11)		(0.04)		(0.17)	
Age	−0.08**	−3	−0.25***	−18	−0.19***	−21
	(0.03)		(0.01)		(0.03)	
Income	0.02	0	−0.053***	−3	0.07	7
	(0.05)		(0.01)		(0.05)	
Education	0.00	−1	0.13***	23	0.081***	18
	(0.02)		(0.01)		(0.02)	
Female	−0.05	0	−0.37***	−6	−0.35***	−8
	(0.08)		(0.03)		(0.09)	

(continued)

TABLE 20 (*continued*)

DV = Support for black candidate	Black	% change	White	% change	Latino	% change
Democrat	0.02 (0.12)	0	−0.44*** (0.03)	−7	−0.52*** (0.12)	−12
Republican	−0.41 (0.26)	−3	0.02 (0.05)	0	−0.02 (0.23)	−1
Southerner	0.21** (0.08)	6	−0.61*** (0.04)	−8	−0.22** (0.11)	−5
Support for other candidate	−5.98*** (0.35)	−21	−1.37*** (0.05)	−18	−2.15*** (0.33)	−24
Delegate surplus/ deficit	0.00 (0.00)	−1	0.00 (0.00)	−1	0.00 (0.00)	−10
Constant	2.13*** (0.32)		−0.40*** (0.11)		−0.12 (0.37)	
Observations	9,494		39,345		2,172	

*Significant at .10, **Significant at .05, ***Significant at .01. Results are derived from three separate logit regressions predicting voter turnout (voted for black candidate in primary election = 1, did not vote for a black candidate in primary election = 0) for each racial/ethnic group.

Chapter 6

TABLE 21. OLS regression predicting perceptions of black candidate racial policy preferences

	Blacks: Candidate prefers government aid to blacks	Whites: Candidate prefers government aid to blacks	Latinos: Candidate prefers government aid to blacks
Jackson (1988)	−0.23 (0.32)	1.02* (0.14)	0.73+ (0.38)
Age	−0.01* (0.01)	−0.00 (0.00)	−0.02* (0.01)
Female	−0.16 (0.18)	−0.06 (0.09)	0.11 (0.17)
Income	−0.09 (0.13)	0.15* (0.06)	−0.16 (0.12)
Education	0.12 (0.13)	0.10+ (0.06)	0.16 (0.12)
Democrat	−0.05 (0.24)	−0.16 (0.13)	−0.13 (0.25)

(*continued*)

TABLE 21 (*continued*)

	Blacks: Candidate prefers government aid to blacks	Whites: Candidate prefers government aid to blacks	Latinos: Candidate prefers government aid to blacks
Republican	1.25*	0.50*	0.43
	(0.60)	(0.12)	(0.35)
Southerner	−0.57	0.18	0.08
	(0.41)	(0.14)	(0.50)
Constant	5.95*	4.84*	5.65*
	(0.54)	(0.23)	(0.58)
Observations	359	1,002	280
R-squared	0.04	0.11	0.09

⁺Significant at .10, *Significant at .05. Standard errors in parentheses. Results are derived from three separate logit regressions predicting perceptions of whether black candidates' support increased government aid to blacks on a seven-point scale.

TABLE 22. Ordered logit regressions predicting perceptions of black candidates' ability to empathize with voters

	Candidate cares about me		
	Blacks	Whites	Latinos
Jackson (1988)	0.62**	−0.09	−0.32
	(0.28)	(0.16)	(0.31)
Age	0.01	−0.01***	−0.02**
	(0.01)	(0.00)	(0.01)
Female	−0.07	0.13	−0.11
	(0.22)	(0.09)	(0.20)
Income	−0.03	−0.26***	−0.03
	(0.14)	(0.06)	(0.14)
Education	0.21	0.04	−0.21
	(0.16)	(0.05)	(0.13)
Democrat	0.52**	0.46***	0.90***
	(0.25)	(0.12)	(0.28)
Republican	0.72	−0.32***	−0.91**
	(0.62)	(0.11)	(0.37)
Southerner	0.12	−0.47***	0.12
	(0.31)	(0.11)	(0.34)

(*continued*)

TABLE 22 (*continued*)

	Candidate cares about me		
	Blacks	Whites	Latinos
Cut 1	−2.93***	−2.25***	−3.02***
	(0.61)	(0.24)	(0.51)
Cut 2	−1.95***	−0.85***	−1.88***
	(0.54)	(0.23)	(0.47)
Cut 3	0.35	1.14***	0.13
	(0.50)	(0.23)	(0.46)
Observations	366	1,608	251

*Significant at .10, **Significant at .05, ***Significant at .01. Standard errors in parentheses. Results are derived from three separate logit regressions predicting perceptions of whether black candidates can empathize with individuals like the respondents.

Notes

Introduction

1. McDevitt 2012.
2. Shirley Chisholm, "Presidential Announcement Speech," Brooklyn, 25 January 1972.
3. Jesse Jackson, "Presidential Announcement Speech," Philadelphia, 16 January 1984.
4. Tate 2010; Johnson 2007.
5. Sonenshein 1990; Strickland and Whicker 1992; Jeffries 1998; Gillespie 2010.
6. Jeffries 1999, 584.
7. Sigelman et al. 1995; Reeves 1997.
8. Susan Page, "Election Tests How Much Race Matters," *USA Today*, 31 October 2006.
9. McIlwain and Caliendo (2011) also investigate the influence racial (positive racial appeals in this study) and racist appeals (negative racial appeals in this study) have on the electorate. However, their examination of racist appeals is focused on white candidates rather than black candidates as is the case in this study. Moreover, our definitions of negative racial appeals differ in that the ones used in this study are used by black candidates in hopes of drawing black support through making claims about unfair treatment, whereas the racist appeals discussed in McIlwain and Caliendo's 2011 study are used by white politicians with the aim of increasing white support through highlighting negative racial stereotypes about black politicians.
10. Hamilton 1977.
11. Bositis 2002; Gillespie 2010.
12. McCormick and Jones 1993.
13. Hamilton 1977; Juenke and Sampaio 2010.
14. Williams 1990.
15. Piston 2010.
16. Sharon D. Wright Austin, and Richard T. Middleton, "The Limitations of the Deracialization Concept in the 2001 Los Angeles Mayoral Election," *Political Research Quarterly* 57(2) (2004): 283–93.; Orey 2006.
17. Cose 2010.
18. Pierannunzi and Hutcheson 1996.
19. Angela K. Lewis, Pearl K. Ford Dowe, and Sekou M. Franklin, "African Americans and Obama's Domestic Policy Agenda: A Closer Look at Deracialization, the Federal Stimulus Bill, and the Affordable Care Act," *Polity* 45 (1) (2013): 127–52.
20. Robnett and Tate 2012.
21. Zeleny 2010.
22. Fenno 1978; Hayes 2005; Funk 1999.

23. Walters 2007; Marable 2009.

24. Gillespie 2012.

25. Curry 2005.

26. Canon, Schousen, and Sellers 1996.

27. Gillespie 2010.

28. Lewis-Beck et al. 2009; Min Baek and Landau 2011; Piston 2010.

29. Lewis-Beck et al. 2009; Min Baek and Landau 2011; Piston 2010.

30. Sweet 1992.

31. Mendelberg 2001; Valentino, Hutchings, and White 2002; Gilens 1999; Peffley and Hurwitz 2007.

32. Sigelman and Todd 1992.

33. Tate 2010; Ford 2008.

34. Ford 2008, 16.

35. Mendelberg 2001; McIlwain and Caliendo 2011.

36. Eugene Rivers, interviewed by Chris Matthews in 2008 on MSNBC's *Hardball*. Retrieved from Web on 15 January 2013.

37. Obama 2006, 247.

38. Orey and Ricks 2007; Jones and Clemmons 1993.

39. Reeves 1997; McIlwain and Caliendo 2011; Krebs and Holian 2007; Metz and Tate 1995; Orey 2006; Terkildsen and Damore 1999.

40. The timeline for this study runs from 1982 to 2010 because state exit polls are not readily available for elections before Tom Bradley's 1982 gubernatorial election, and no black candidate campaigned for high-profile statewide election in 2012.

41. Alan Keyes (R-MD, 1988), Troy Brown (D-MS., 2000), and Wayne Sowell (D-AL, 2004) were excluded for not having at least forty articles in which their name appeared. Barack Obama (D-IL, 2004) and Alan Keyes (R-IL, 2004) were excluded because they did not face white opponents.

42. While I use newspapers to assess levels of racialization in a campaign, future research should reexamine my results using content analysis of other forms of media. While there is a significant overlap in coverage between television and print media, research shows that viewers of television media retain different types of information than readers of print media (Chaffee and Frank 1996). Moreover, future researchers may want to reassess the results of this study by conducting content analysis of entertainment news and social media outlets such as Facebook and Twitter.

43. Druckman 2005.

44. Hamilton 2004.

45. Dalton, Beck, and Huckfeldt 1998.

46. Reeves 1997; McIlwain and Caliendo 2011; Metz and Tate 1995; Krebs and Holian 2007; Orey 2006; Terkildsen and Damore 1999.

47. I ran a separate model with a broader definition of the candidate's staff that included staffers and Democratic or Republican party members. The results presented in the following chapters do not change significantly with the inclusion of this broader racialization measure. However, many of these comments are included in the model through the media racialization control.

48. Thus, even if the candidate made numerous racial appeals as reported in an article, the highest score an article could receive was a 2 for positive racial appeals and a 1 for negative racial appeals.

49. A 10 percent sample of the articles was coded by a second individual. Based on their coding, agreement on all five measures was over 90 percent. Cohen's kappa score for positive racialization (.67), negative racialization (1), opponent negative racialization (.83), opponent positive racialization (.86), and media racialization (.78) are all within Landis and Koch's (1977) substantial agreement range.

50. I use an additive scale rather than examine implicit and explicit appeals separately. While this approach may provide a less detailed understanding of whether different types of appeals influence vote choice, by disaggregating these two measure we lose the ability to examine the total racialization of the election. Given that implicit and explicit racial appeals are not made in a vacuum and are highly correlated, it is difficult to distinguish which appeals voters are responding to most when we separate these measures. A test of this relationship would be better suited for an experimental setting. For those interested in this topic, I estimated separate models accounting for the percent of implicit and/or explicit racial appeals as predictors of vote choice and turnout. Ultimately, the results showed that both explicit and implicit racial appeals improve black candidates' standing among black voters and do not diminish their support among whites. Surprisingly, Latinos are more supportive of black candidates who utilize more positive explicit appeals. Neither implicit nor explicit positive racial appeals influence turnout for any of the racial/ethnic groups.

51. Some issues straddle the line between being explicitly and implicitly racial. For example, felon disenfranchisement and welfare may be more racially tinged than issues such as minimum wage. Some may even argue that issues such as welfare are explicitly racial (see Edsall and Edsall 1992). While a number of coding schemes could be created, I decide to define explicit racial appeals as only those issues which directly mention or entail race. I did, however, try alternate coding schemes that placed all racial appeals on the same scale. The results of this analysis do not provide different results than those presented in the text. That being said, I hope future research reassesses the results in this book with alternate coding schemes.

52. Mendelberg 2001; Huber and Lapinski 2008; Valentino, Hutchings, and White 2002; Gilens 1999; Peffley and Hurwitz 2007; Christie 2013; Metz and Tate 1995; and McIlwain and Caliendo 2011.

53. Gillman and Jeffers 2002.

54. Metz and Tate 1995.

55. While disregarding race is not a racial appeal, it still brings attention to race. A measure of media racialization, which is used in chapters 2 and 3 and described in the appendix, creates a control to account for the injection of race without the intent of appealing to black voters.

56. Jordan and Melton 1988.

57. Sher 2008.

58. Schelzig 2006a.

59. Ford and Glaser 2010, 223.

60. Charlie Mitchell, "Democrats Being Practical, Not Racist," *Enterprise-Journal*, 10 September 2008, Opinion Section.

61. "Today's Quote," *Charlotte Observer*, 28 September 1990, 2C.

62. Taylor 1988.

63. Scoppe 1990.

64. The 1988 American National Election Study used in the analysis for voter turnout in chapter 4 has too few Latino respondents to make statistical comparisons.

1. What Are My Choices?

1. "Obama for U.S. Senate," editorial, *State Journal-Register*, 29 October 2004, 8.

2. "Forum," *Topeka Capital-Journal*, 29 July 2004.

3. "Alan Keyes Lights 'em Up," *Chicago Tribune*, 14 September 2004, B1.

4. "IL: Keyes Compares Abortion to Terrorism," *Frontrunner*, 17 August 2004.

5. Cathleen Falsani, "How Would Jesus Vote? Keyes Can't Presume to Know," *Chicago Sun-Times*, 10 September 2004, P32.

6. See Strickland and Whicker 1992; Sonenshein 1990; and Jeffries 1999.

7. The focus in this chapter is disaggregating black *candidates* by their use of racial appeals. See Gillespie 2010 for an excellent categorization of black *elected officials* and racialization.

8. U.S. Census, 2010, file 1, prepared by the U.S. Census Bureau, 2011.

9. See Grofman and Handley 1989; Lublin 1997.

10. McCormick and Jones 1993; Perry 1996; Wright 1996.

11. Jeffries 1999, 585.

12. Sigelman et al. 1995; Reeves 1997; Terkildsen 1993.

13. Strickland and Whicker 1992; Sonenshein 1990; and Jeffries 1999.

14. Lewis-Beck et al. 2009.

15. Huntington Williams, "Taking Helms by the Tarheel," *Washington Post*, 21 October 1990, C1.

16. Gilliam and Kaufman 1998.

17. Abby Goodnough, "Patrick Hangs On as Massachusetts Governor," *New York Times*, 3 November 2010.

18. William Francis Galvin, "Massachusetts Registered Voter Enrollment: 1948–2012," Massachusetts Secretary of State, retrieved from www.sec.state.ma.us/ele/eleenr/enridx .htm, accessed 30 March 2014.

19. The central tunnel artery project, also known as the "Big Dig," was a construction project that hoped to alleviate traffic in Boston by creating a number of new highways and tunnels. The unpopular project was plagued by higher than expected costs and a number of delays.

20. Schelzig 2006b.

21. Keen 2006.

22. Navarrette 2002.

23. Ratcliffe 2002.

24. Gillman and Jeffers 2002.

25. Jeffers 2002.

26. Greenson 2009.

27. Cardon 1986.

28. Shaughnessy 1986.

29. Byers 1986.

30. Scoppe 1990.

31. Surratt 1990.

32. "Campbell Enjoys a Large Lead," *Herald Journal*, 7 October 1990.

33. Faler 2002.

34. Vogel 2002.

35. Neff 2002.

36. Neff 2002.

37. Vogel 2002.

2. Black Candidates and Voter Turnout

1. Pickler 2007.

2. Benjamin 2002.

3. Preston 1983; Bobo and Gilliam 1990; Tate 1991.

4. Keele and White 2011.

5. McDermott 1998; Washington 2006.

6. Tate 2003.

7. Griffin and Keane 2006.

8. Tate 1991; McKenzie 2004; Secret et al. 1990; Philpot, Shaw, and McGowen 2009; Uhlaner 1989a, 1989b; Rosenstone and Hansen 1993.

9. Mendelberg 2001; McIlwain and Caliendo 2011; Tate 2012.

10. Ham and Carroll 1990.

11. Washington 2006; Reeves 1997; Gay 2001.

12. Reeves 1997.

13. Bobo and Kluegel 1993, 1996; Kinder and Sanders 1996.

14. Summers and Klinkner 1990.

15. Gillespie 2010.

16. Jesse Jackson, "Presidential Announcement Speech," Philadelphia, 16 January 1984.

17. Kaufmann 2003; Vaca 2004; McClain and Karnig 1990.

18. McClain et al. 2006.

19. These graphs and subsequent models exclude the 2008 cases, as Obama's effect on black turnout may confound the results.

20. U.S. Census 2006. United States Department of Commerce. Bureau of the Census, United States Department of Labor. Bureau of Labor Statistics, and United States Department of Commerce. Bureau of the Census. Housing and Household Economic Statistics Division. Current Population Survey, November 2006: Voting and Registration Supplement. ICPSR21340-v2. Ann Arbor, MI: Inter-university Consortium for Political and Social Research, 2011–02–07.

21. Silver, Anderson, and Abramson 1986; Presser 1990; Ansolabehere and Hersh 2012.

22. McKee, Hood, and Hill 2012.

23. Silver, Anderson, and Abramson 1986; Berent, Krosnick, and Lupia 2011.

24. Holbrook and Krosnick 2010.

25. While there is no evidence to suggest that the racial context of an election would influence social desirability response bias, the possibility exists. Unfortunately, there were too few black candidates who campaigned for high-profile statewide office in years where surveys had vote-validated data at the time this book was written. Future research should reassess the results of this study using vote-validated data as it becomes available.

26. See table 13 in the appendix for detailed information about the candidates used in this analysis and sample size in each election.

27. An alternate approach may be to examine voter turnout files from secretary of state's offices around the country. This would allow for a more direct examination of voter turnout in elections with high-profile statewide candidates. In particular, it is possible that some people who said that they voted only participated in the presidential election and not in the election with the high-profile statewide candidate of interest. As a result, these voters would

be over counted as voting in the election with the black candidate in my models. However, many states do not record information about voters' race or ethnicity. In fact, only nine states in their entirety collect information about the voters' race due to restrictions placed by section 5 of the 1965 Voting Right Act. Thus an examination of state's official turnout records would allow for an analysis of changes in turnout for the electorate as a whole, but would not allow for an exploration of voters of different races/ethnicities.

In the previous chapter I disaggregated candidates based partly on their use of racial appeals, but in the analysis conducted in this and the following chapter, I choose to use a continuous measure of racialization, the average article's positive or negative racial appeal score, rather than examine the candidates by categories. I believe this provides a more nuanced assessment of racialization by increasing the amount of variation in my independent variables of interest. For example, if I used a dichotomous variable such as for the Racialized Rule Follower group, the positive racial appeals scores for these candidates which range from .09 for Harold Ford (D-TN, 2006) to .29 for Michael Steele (R-MD, 2006) would all be given the same score (i.e., 1 for the dichotomous Racialized Rule Follower variable). While I do not perform this analysis in the book, a separate analysis not reported used the categories created in chapter 2 to assess how different black candidates influence the electorate. Similar to the results presented in table 4, the candidates who are the most viable, the Nonracialized Rule Followers, are the only candidates who increase black turnout at a greater rate than their de-racialized counterparts. Moreover, black candidates who use the most racial appeals (i.e., Racialized Rule Followers and Racialized Longshots) do not have any influence on black turnout.

28. While these candidates play a large role in influencing my analysis of negative racial appeals and turnout, alternate coding specifications used to address this skewed variable including using the log transformation of the negative racialization score and coding the variable into quartiles rather than on a continuous scale yield statistically similar results as the continuous measures of negative racialization presented in table 4 and used in the analysis in both this and the following chapter. As a result, even limiting the influence of these outliers does not yield radically different results.

29. Too few Asian Americans were surveyed to conduct a meaningful analysis about their participation rates.

30. See the appendix for the content coding of the media and opponents' levels of racialization

31. Squire's 1992 index gives scores of 6 to candidates who had previously held the position of governor or U.S. senator or is an incumbent, 5 for U.S. House representatives, 4 for statewide elected officials, 3 for state legislators, 2 for local elected officials, 1 for nonelected positions (e.g., party chair), and 0 for those who held no political office. These scores are then multiplied by the percentage of the state's population that the individual represented.

32. This measure is constructed by dividing the candidate's campaign spending totals by the opponent's disbursement totals. For example, candidates who spent twice as much as their opponent received a score of 2. However, if the candidates only spent half as much as their opponent, they received a score of .5.

33. This is measured by taking the difference between the state's average levels of support for the most recent Democratic presidential candidate and the Democratic presidential candidate's national level of support. This measure was multiplied by −1 if the candidate of interest is a Republican.

34. In addition to controlling for the difference in the culture in the South, this measure also serves as a proxy for the size of the black population. In 2010, 55 percent of the black population resided in the South (2010 U.S. Census)

35. The nested nature of this data raises the possibility of non-independence among respondents. In particular, voters in the same state and in the same year may be more similar than different with regard to their likelihood of voting. If this occurs, the results could be biased. Each model corrects for this possibility using robust standard errors that are clustered for state-years.

36. This is calculated by examining the change in the dependent variable when the independent variable of interest changes from its minimum to its maximum level and all other variables at held at their mean values.

37. The results do not vary if the racialization measures are coded dichotomously rather than on a three-point scale. Thus the results are not contingent on the racialization measures being coded on a three-point rather than a two-point scale. Moreover, neither implicit nor explicit positive racial appeals have any influence on black turnout.

38. Vanderleeuw et al. 2004; Pierannunzi and Hutcheson 1996; Summers and Klinkner 1996; Wright 1996.

39. Lublin 1999.

3. Racializing and Winning Elections

1. Strong 1990.

2. "Campbell Enjoys a Large Lead," *Herald Journal*, 7 October 1990.

3. "Why Ron Sims Is Best Choice," *Seattle Post-Intelligencer*, 3 November 1994, A10.

4. Citrin, Green, and Sears 1990; Orey 2006; Pierannunzi and Hutcheson 1996; Swain 1993.

5. McIlwain and Caliendo 2011; Tate 2012.

6. Bositis 2010.

7. Ham and Carroll 1990.

8. Vanderleeuw et al. 2004.

9. Pierannunzi and Hutcheson 1996.

10. Schmich 1990.

11. King-Meadows 2010.

12. Walters 2007; Marable 2009.

13. Serwer 2008; "Panic Mode: The Clinton Campaign Stoops to Sleazy Tactics," *Pittsburgh Post-Gazette*, 22 December 2007.

14. Orey 2006.

15. Carmines and Stimson 1980; Goren 1997; Abrajano and Alvarez 2005.

16. Citrin, Green, and Sears 1990; Perry 1996.

17. Citrin, Green, and Sears 1990; Terkildsen 1993; Sigelman et al. 1995; Reeves 1997.

18. Mendelberg 2001; McIlwain and Caliendo 2011; Valentino, Hutchings, and White 2002.

19. Nelson, Sanbonmatsu, and McClerking 2007.

20. Skocpol 1991; Perry 2011.

21. DeSipio 1996; Garcia 2003.

22. Schildkraut 2005; Masuoka 2006.

23. Kaufmann 2003; Vaca 2004; McClain and Karnig 1990.

24. See table 16 in the appendix for detailed information about the number of respondents in each exit poll and the organization responsible for administering the exit polls.

25. Again, alternate model specifications in which the racialization measure is logged or coded into four categories are used to limit the influence of outliers in these measures. Ultimately, these models do not produce drastically different results from those presented in table 5 in the text.

26. The results do not vary if the racialization measures are coded dichotomously rather than on a three-point scale.

27. The results do not vary if the dichotomous dependent variable compares only black candidates to their major party rivals.

28. This is measured by taking the difference between the state's average levels of support for the most recent Democratic presidential candidate and the Democratic presidential candidate's national level of support. This measure was multiplied by −1 if the candidate of interest is a Republican.

29. One of the main problems with the exit polls is that they do not consistently ask the same demographic and political questions across all years. In particular, only some exit polls ask questions about the respondents' level of education or their political ideology. Given the already limited number of elections that are included in this study, I exclude these variables from the analysis.

30. As with the models presented in chapter 2, this analysis includes robust standard errors that account for the statistical non-independence of individuals in the same election.

31. In a separate analysis, I used the categories created in chapter 1 to assess black candidates' effect on the electorate. Similar to the results in table 5, black candidates who utilize the most positive racial appeals are the only groups who achieve significantly higher levels of support from the black electorate than those in the Go Quietly category. Thus, regardless of how racialization is coded, candidates who are associated with positive racial appeals generally receive the highest levels of support among black voters. Moreover, black candidates who are associated with positive racial appeals did not lose support among whites or Latinos. In fact, no category of black candidates significantly differed in their levels of support from white or Latino voters when other factors are held constant.

32. In a separate analysis, I estimated the influence that implicit and explicit racial appeals had on vote choice. Similar to the results in table 5, blacks were significantly more supportive of black candidates who made either implicit or explicit racial appeals. Explicit positive racial appeals, however, were the only racial appeals that increased support from Latino voters. Neither positive implicit nor explicit racial appeals influenced vote choice among white voters. Thus even explicit positive racial appeals do not dampen white support for black candidates.

33. Vanderleeuw et al. 2004; Pierannunzi and Hutcheson 1996; Summers and Klinkner 1996; Wright 1996.

34. Pierannunzi and Hutcheson 1996; Summers and Klinkner 1996; Orey 2006.

4. The First Black President

1. Younge 2007.
2. Royko 1988.
3. *Arkansas Democrat-Gazette*, 24 February 1988.
4. Marelius 1988.
5. Orange County Register, 15 March 1988, A6.
6. O'Brien 1988.
7. Hepburn 1988.

8. Brummer 1988.

9. Dillin 1988.

10. Harris 2012.

11. Mooney 2008.

12. Maddaus 2008.

13. Ross 2008.

14. Mary Mitchell 2008.

15. Hurt 2008.

16. Zeleny and Hulse 2008.

17. There are not a sufficient number of Latino voters to draw any conclusion about their voting behaviors in 1988.

18. The results only include Democrats because some states hold closed primaries that disqualify some voters from participating in the election. To standardize the comparison across states, I limit my sample to Democratic respondents.

19. The results of logistic regression analysis that controls for age, income, education, gender, region, and differences in the black candidate's pledged delegate lead relative to their opponent also demonstrate that black turnout did not significantly differ in either the 1988 or 2008 Democratic presidential primaries. However, similar to the results in table 6, white turnout was significantly lower in 1988 when compared to 2008. See table 19 in the appendix for more details.

20. Gherson 1988.

21. The differences between black, white, and Latino support for Jackson compared with Obama reported in table 7 remains significant and in the same direction in logit regression analysis that includes a number of controls including age, income, education, gender, region, and differences in the black candidate's pledged delegate lead relative to the opponent. See table 20 in the appendix for more details.

22. Marsh 1985; McAllister and Studlar 1991.

23. Dionne 1988.

24. Walker 2008.

5. Positive and Negative Racial Appeals in Action

1. Moreover, given that very few black U.S. Senate and gubernatorial candidates use negative racial appeals, more research is necessary to show that voters' reactions to negative racial appeals are not simply the results of a skewed negative racialization variable.

2. Brian Ross, "Reverend Jeremiah Wright, Obama's Pastor Now a Campaign Liability?" ABC News, 13 March 2008.

3. Walker and Smithers 2009.

4. Jim Vandehei and John Harris, "Race Uproar Offers Test for Obama," Politico.com, 17 March 2008.

5. Jim Farber, "Geraldine Ferraro Lets Her Emotions Do the Talking," *Daily Breeze*, 7 March 2008.

6. Vandehei and Harris 2008.

7. Crouch 2006; Serwer 2008.

8. Obama, 2008.

9. Sigelman and Welch 1994.

10. Tate 2010.

11. Ari Melber, "Obama's Speech Makes YouTube History," *Nation*, 15 March 2008.

12. Pew Research Center, "Obama Speech on Race Arguably Biggest Event of Campaign," http://pewresearch.org/pubs/777/obama-wright-news-interest.

13. Dalia Sussman, "Poll: Obama Receives High Marks for Race Speech," *New York Times*, 21 March 2008.

14. Bill Richardson, "Remarks by Governor Bill Richardson on His Endorsement of Senator Barack Obama for President," Memorial Coliseum, Portland, Oregon. 21 March 2008.

15. *PBS NewsHour*, "Obama Speech Opens Discourse on Race and Politics," 18 March 2008.

16. Cable News Network, "Analysts: Obama Speech Achieved Goal," 18 March 2008.

17. Robert Press, "Problem for Jackson Campaign: How to Woo White Voters," *Christian Science Monitor*, 17 January 1984.

18. Howell Raines, "Jackson Coup and the 84 Race," *New York Times*, 4 January 1984.

19. Barry Sussman, "Polls See Debate Aiding Mondale, Jackson Most," *Washington Post*, 17 January 1984.

20. "Glenn, Jackson Tied for Second Spot behind Mondale, Gallup Poll Shows," *Washington Post*, 17 February 1984, A4.

21. Barker 1988.

22. Donald M. Rothberg, "Jackson Acknowledges Calling Jews 'Hymies,'" Associated Press, 26 February 1984.

23. Matthew Quinn, "Jackson: Campaign Being 'Persecuted,'" United Press International, 21 February 1984.

24. Michael Hirschorn, "Candidate Watch: Jesse and the Jews," *Harvard Crimson*, 5 March 1984.

25. William Ries, United Press International, 26 February 1984.

26. Russ, Valeria Russ, "JDL Threat Overlooked, Muslim Says." *Philadelphia Daily News*, 5 March 1984.

27. Richard Cohen, 1984. "Bias; Perhaps Jackson Will Prove Educable on the Subject of Jews," *Washington Post*, 22 February 1984.

28. The national election pool is a conglomeration of news organizations including ABC News, CBS News, NBC News, CNN, Fox News, and the Associated Press. Twenty-two primaries and caucuses occurred after Super Tuesday, but exit polls were only available for fifteen. The following states were used in this analysis: IN, KY, LA, MD, MS, MT, NC, OH, OR, PA, RI, SD, TX, VA, WI.

29. The results for our independent variable of interest (primary occurred after the More Perfect Union speech) do not change for any racial/ethnic groups if I do not restrict the comparison primary dates to after Super Tuesday. In fact, the magnitude of the effect of the speech on black and Latino support for Obama is greater if the comparison group includes respondents in all primaries rather than just including those who resided in states whose primaries occurred after Super Tuesday. Thus the results presented in tables 8 and 9 in some ways understate the relationship between positive racial appeals and voter support.

30. Only the Iowa caucus had occurred at this point in 1984. The exit polls for the caucus include too few African Americans to make a meaningful comparison about Jackson's support before or after the Hymietown controversy.

31. Tate 1993.

6. Who Cares?

1. See Mendelberg 2001; McIlwain and Caliendo 2011.

2. McIlwain and Caliendo 2011.

3. Vanderleeuw et al. 2004.

4. Herr 2002; Hill, Rodriquez, and Wooden 2010.

5. Castro 2002.

6. Hammer 2008.

7. Carmines and Stimson 1980; Goren 1997; Abrajano and Alvarez 2005.

8. Jeffries 1999; Reeves 1997; Terkildsen 1993.

9. Lewis-Beck et al. 2009; Min Baek and Landau 2011; Piston 2010.

10. Susswein 2002.

11. All of the same relationships in the comparison of means test between Obama and Jackson displayed in figure 5 remain the same in terms of significance and direction in an OLS regression model that controls for age, income, education, partisanship, and region (e.g., South). See table 21 in the appendix for these results.

12. In the 2008 ANES, only half of respondents were asked how much the candidate cares about them on a four-point scale. The other respondents in the 2008 ANES were asked this question using a five-point scale. For the sake of consistency, I only compare respondents in the 2008 data set who were asked the question using the same four-point scale as the 1988 data set in the analysis presented in figure 6. An alternate specification that standardized all scores to make comparisons of respondents measured on different scales provided the same result. Namely, blacks were significantly more likely to believe that Jackson cared about them in 1988 than Obama in 2008.

13. All of the same relationships in the chi-square test between Obama and Jackson displayed in figure 6 remain the same in terms of significance in an ordered logit regression model that controls for age, income, education, partisanship, and region (e.g., South). See table 22 in the conclusion for these results.

14. Using the same metric for positive racialization discussed in the introduction, the author performed a content analysis of a random sample of one hundred articles for Barack Obama and Jesse Jackson from 1 January of the election year until the last primary date.

15. Berman 2012.

16. Lewis-Beck et al. 2009; Piston 2010; Min Baek and Landau 2011.

Conclusion

1. Cose 2010.

2. Dawson 1994; Tate 1993; Gillespie 2012.

3. Belinda Robnett and Katherine Tate, "Outlook on Life and Political Engagement," 31 December 2012.

4. According to CNN exit polls, Obama only received 43 percent of the white vote in 2008 and 39 percent in 2012.

5. Dahl 1961; Clark 1975; Erie 1978.

6. Gillespie quoted in Cobb 2012.

7. Bobo and Gilliam 1990; Tate 2003; Abney and Hutcheson 1981; Griffin and Keane 2006; Stout and Le 2012.

8. Philpot and Walton 2009.

9. Terkildsen 1993; Hunter 2013; Weaver 2012.

10. Hunter 2013.

Bibliography

Abney, Glenn F., and John D. Hutcheson Jr. 1981. "Race, Representation, and Trust: Changes in Attitudes after the Election of a Black Mayor." *Public Opinion Quarterly* 45(1): 91–101.

Abrajano, Marissa, and R. Michael Alvarez. 2005. "A Natural Experiment of Race-Based and Issue Voting: The 2001 City of Los Angeles Elections." *Political Research Quarterly* 58(2): 203–18.

Ansolabehere, Stephen, and Eitan Hersh. 2012. "Validation: What Big Data Reveal about Survey Misreporting and the Real Electorate." *Political Analysis* 20(4): 437–59.

Absolabehere, Stephen, Shanto Iyengar, Adam Simon, and Nicholas Valentino. 1994. "Does Attack Advertising Demobilize the Electorate?" *American Political Science Review* 88(4):829–38.

Ansolabehere, Stephen, and Philip Edward Jones. 2010. "Constituents' Responses to Congressional Roll-Call Voting." *American Journal of Political Science* 54(3): 583–97.

Barker, Lucius J. 1988. *Our Time Has Come: A Delegate's Diary of Jesse Jackson's 1984 Presidential Campaign.* Urbana: University of Illinois Press.

Barreto, Matt, Luis Fraga, Sylvia Manzano, Valerie Martinez-Ebers, and Gary Segura. 2008. "Should They Dance with the One Who Brung 'em? Latinos and the 2008 Presidential Election." *PS: Political Science & Politics* 41(3): 753–60.

Benjamin, Gerald. 2002. "Who'd Want to Govern New York State?" *New York Times,* 3 September, A1.

Berent, Matthew K., Jon A. Krosnick, and Arthur Lupia. 2011. "The Quality of Government Records and Over-estimation of Registration and Turnout in Surveys: Lessons from the 2008 ANES Panel Study's Registration and Turnout Validation Exercises." Working Paper no. nes012554. Ann Arbor and Palo Alto: American National Election Studies. Available at http://www.electionstudies.org/resources/papers/nes012554.

Berman, Dan. 2012. "Mitt Romney: President Obama Won Because of 'Gifts.'" *Politico.* Retrieved from http://www.politico.com/news/stories/1112/83878.html on 7/10/2013

Bobo, Lawrence, and Franklin Gilliam. 1990. "Race, Sociopolitical Participation, and Black Empowerment." *American Political Science Review* 84(2): 377–39.

Bobo, Lawrence, and Vincent L. Hutchings. 1996. "Perceptions of Racial Group Competition: Extending Blumer's Theory of Group Position to a Multiracial Social Context." *American Sociological Review* 61(6): 951–72.

Bobo, Lawrence, and James Kluegel. 1993. "Opposition to Race-Targeting: Self-Interest, Stratification Ideology, or Racial Attitudes." *American Sociological Review* 58(3): 443–64.

Borges, Jesse. 1988. "Beyond Deracialization: Towards a Comprehensive Theory of Black Electoral Success." PhD diss., Princeton University.

Bositis, David. 2002. "Latest Report of Black Elected Officials: A Statistical Summary." Washington, D.C.: Joint Center for Political and Economic Studies.

———. 2010. "The Political Orientations of Young African Americans." In *Barack Obama and African American Empowerment: The Rise of Black America's New Leadership,* ed. Manning Marable and Kristin Clarke. New York: Palgrave-Macmillan.

Brummer, Alex. 1988. "Power or Glory? Although Jesse Jackson Has Lost New York, He Has Emerged as Possible Kingmaker for the Democrats." *Guardian,* 21 April.

Byers, Jim. 1986. "Californians Face Tough Choices." *Toronto Star,* 21 September, B3.

Canon, David T., Matthew M. Schousen, and Patrick J. Sellers. 1996. "The Supply Side of Congressional Redistricting: Race and Strategic Politicians, 1972–1992." *Journal of Politics* 58(3): 846–62.

Cardon, Daniel. 1986. "Deukmejian Assisting GOP Hopefuls with Funds." *San Diego Union Tribune,* 2 November, A1.

Carmines, Edward, and James Stimson. 1980. "The Two Faces of Issue Voting." *American Political Science Review* 74(1): 78–91.

Castro, April. 2002. "Hip-Hop Performers Rally for Kirk—Def Jam Founder Gives His Support." *San Antonio Express-News,* 16 October, 8B.

Census Summary, 2010, file 1, prepared by the U.S. Census Bureau, 2011.

Chaffee, Steven, and Stacey Frank. 1996. "How Americans Get Political Information: Print versus Broadcast News." *Annals of the American Academy of Political and Social Science* 546(1): 48–58.

Christie, Natasha. 2013. "Racial Neutrality by Any Other Name: An Examination of Collateral Consequence Policies in the United States. *Social Science Quarterly,* 15 April.

Citrin, Jack, Donald Phillip Green, and David O. Sears. 1990. "White Reactions to Black Candidates: When Does Race Matter?" *Public Opinion Quarterly* 54(1): 74–96

Clark, Terry. 1975. "The Irish Ethic and the Spirit of Patronage." *Ethnicity* 2(1): 305–59.

Cobb, William Jelani. 2010. *The Substance of Hope: Barack Obama and the Paradox of Progress.* New York: Bloomsbury.

———. 2012. "Cory Booker: The Dilemma of the New Black Politician." *New Yorker,* 22 May.

Collet, Christian. 2008. "Minority Candidates, Alternative Media, and Multiethnic America: Deracialization or Toggling?" *Perspective on Politics* 6(4): 707–28.

Cose, Ellis. 2010. "Fallen Star." *Daily Beast,* 3 June. http://www.newsweek.com/why -alabama-artur-davis-lost-black-vote-73079.

Crouch, Stanley. 2006. "What Obama Isn't: Black Like Me on Race." *New York Daily News,* 2 November, 35.

Curry, Marshall. 2005. *Street Fight.* Oley: Bullfrog Films.

Dahl, Robert. 1961. *Who Governs.* New Haven: Yale University Press.

Dalton, Russell J., Paul A. Beck, and Robert Huckfeldt. 1998. "Partisan Cues and the Media: Information Flows in the 1992 Presidential Election." *American Political Science Review* 92(1): 111–26.

Dawson, Michael. 1994. *Behind the Mule.* Princeton: Princeton University Press.

DeSipio, Louis. 1996. *Counting on the Latino Vote: Latinos as a New Electorate.* Charlottesville: University of Virginia Press.

Dillin, John. 1988. "Speculation Heats Up on Vice-President Slot—Who and What Role? Jackson Going Only for No. 1, an Adviser Says." *Christian Science Monitor,* 26 April, 5.

Dionne, E. J., Jr. 1988. Poll Shows Dukakis Leads Bush; Many Reagan Backers Shift Sides. *New York Times,* 17 May.

Druckman, Jamie. 2005. "Media Matter: How Newspapers and Television News Cover Campaigns and Influence Voters." *Political Communication* 22(4): 463–81.

Edsall, Thomas Byrne, and Mary D. Edsall. 1992. *Chain Reaction.* New York: W. W. Norton.

Erie, Steven. 1978. "Politics, the Public Sector, and Irish Social Mobility: San Francisco, 1870–1900." *Western Political Quarterly* 31(2): 274–89.

Faler, Brian. 2002. "For Illinois GOP, It's a Bad Year to Run a Ryan." *Washington Post,* 5 September, A9.

Fenno, Richard. 1978. *Homestyle: House Members in Their Districts.* White Plains: Longman.

———. 2003. *Going Home: Black Representatives and Their Constituents.* Chicago: University of Chicago Press.

Finn, Christopher, and Jack Glaser. 2010. "Voter Affect and the 2008 U.S. Presidential Election: Hope and Race Mattered." *Analyses of Social Issues and Public Policy* 10(1): 262–75.

Ford, Harold, Jr. 2010. *More Davids than Goliaths: A Political Education.* New York: Random House Digital.

Ford, Richard Thompson. 2008. *The Race Card: How Bluffing about Bias Makes Race Relations Worse.* New York: Macmillan.

Franklin, Sekou. 2010. "Situational Deracialization, Harold Ford, and the 2006 Senate Race in Tennessee." In *Whose Black Politics? Cases in Post-Racial Black Leadership,* ed. Andra Gillespie. New York: Routledge.

Frederick, Kristofer A., and Judson L. Jeffries. 2009. "A Study in African American Candidates for High-Profile Statewide Office." *Journal of Black Studies* 39(5): 689–719.

Funk, Carolyn L. 1999. "Bringing the Candidate into Models of Candidate Evaluation." *Journal of Politics* 61(3): 700–720.

Garcia, John. 2003. *Latino Politics in America: Community, Culture, and Interests.* Lanham: Rowman and Littlefield.

Gay, Claudine. 2001. "The Effect of Black Congressional Representation on Political Participation." *American Political Science Review* 95(3): 589–602.

Gherson, Giles. 1988. "N.Y. Democrats Have a Week to Make Up Minds." *Financial Post,* April 13.

Gilens, Martin. 1999. *Why Americans Hate Welfare: Race, Media, and the Politics of Antipoverty Strategy.* Chicago: University of Chicago Press.

Gillespie, Andra. 2010. "Meet the New Class: Theorizing Young Black Leadership in a Postracial Era." In *Whose Black Politics? Cases in Post-Racial Black Leadership,* ed. Andra Gillespie. New York: Routledge.

———. 2012. *The New Black Politician: Cory Booker, Newark, and Post-Racial America.* New York: New York University Press.

Gilliam, F. D., Jr., and K. M. Kaufmann. 1998. "Is There an Empowerment Life Cycle? Long-Term Black Empowerment and Its Influence on Voter Participation." *Urban Affairs Review* 33(6): 741.

Gillman, Todd J., and Gromer Jeffers Jr. 2002. "Hopefuls Energized at Home—As Kirk Gets Backing of LBJ Clan, Veterans Rally around Cornyn." *Dallas Morning News,* 30 October, 1A.

Glaser, James M. 1988 *Race, Campaign Politics, and the Realignment in the South.* New Haven: Yale University Press.

Goren, Paul. 1997. "Political Expertise and Issue Voting in Presidential Elections." *Political Research Quarterly* 50(2): 387–412.

Greenson, Thadeus. 2009. "State Lawmakers Approval Ratings Take a Dive." *Times Standard,* 16 October. http://www.times-standard.com/localnews/ci_13575368. Accessed 1 June 2012.

Griffin, John D., and Michael Keane. 2006. "Descriptive Representation and the Composition of African American Turnout." *American Journal of Political Science* 50(4): 998–1012.

Grofman, Bernard, and Lisa Handley. 1989. "Minority Population Proportion and Black and Hispanic Congressional Success in the 1970s and 1980s." *American Politics Quarterly* 17(4): 436–45.

Hajnal, Zoltan. 2001. "White Residents, Black Incumbents, and a Declining Racial Divide." *American Political Science Review* 95(3): 603–17.

———. 2007. *Changing White Attitudes toward Black Political Leadership.* Cambridge: Cambridge University Press.

Ham, Faith Lyman, and Chuck Carroll. 1990. "Mitchell Remarks Sparks Flurry of Activity." *Herald-Journal,* 29 September.

Hamilton, Charles. 1977. "Deracialization: Examination of a Political Strategy." *First World,* March/April, 3–5.

Hamilton, James. 2004. *All the News That's Fit to Shell: How the Market Transforms Information into News.* Princeton: Princeton University Press.

Hammer, David. 2008. "Nation's Black Leaders Gather in New Orleans." *Times Picayune,* 23 February.

Harris, Frederick C. 2012. *The Price of the Ticket: Barack Obama and Rise and Decline of Black Politics*. New York: Oxford University Press.

Hayes, Danny. 2005. "Candidate Qualities through a Partisan Lens: A Theory of Trait Ownership." *American Journal of Political Science* 49(4): 908–23.

Hepburn, Bob. 1988. "Jackson's Leftism Causes Jitters in U.S." *Toronto Star*, 9 April, D1.

Hero, Rodney, and Robert Preuhs. 2009. "Beyond (the Scope of) Conflict National Black and Latino Advocacy Relations in the Congressional and Legal Arenas." *Perspectives on Politics* 7(3): 501–17.

Herr, J. Paul. 2002. "The Impact of Campaign Appearances in the 1996 Election." *Journal of Politics* 64(3): 904–13.

Highton, Benjamin. 2004. "White Voters and African American Candidates for Congress." *Political Behavior* 26(1): 1–25.

Hill, Jeffrey, Elaine Rodriquez, and Amanda E Wooden. 2010. "Stump Speeches and Road Trips: The Impact of State Campaign Appearances in Presidential Elections." *PS: Political Science & Politics* 43(2): 243–54.

Holbrook, Allyson L., and Jon A. Krosnick. 2010. "Social Desirability Bias in Voter Turnout Reports Tests Using the Item Count Technique." *Public Opinion Quarterly* 74(1): 37–67.

Huber, Gregory A., and John S. Lapinski. 2006. "The 'Race Card' Revisited: Assessing Racial Priming in Policy Contests." *American Journal of Political Science* 50(2): 421–40.

———. 2008. "Testing the Implicit-Explicit Model of Racialized Political Communication." *Perspectives on Politics* 6(1): 125–34.

Hunter, Margaret L. 2013. *Race, Gender, and the Politics of Skin Tone*. New York: Routledge.

Hurt, Charles. 2008. "Jesse Jackson Says He Wants to Cut Obama's 'Nuts Out.'" *New York Post*, 14 November. http://www.nypost.com/p/news/national/item_2IKMVtS3vzx RvoAAxZoZGL.

Jeffers, Gromer. 2002. "At Hip-Hop Summit, Kirk Pleads for Generation to Vote; In Audience, Green Party Hopeful Criticizes Democrat's Record." *Dallas Morning News*, 13 October, 33A.

Jeffries, Judson. 1999. "U.S. Senator Edward W. Brooke and Governor L. Douglas Wilder Tell Political Scientists How Blacks Can Win High-Profile Statewide Office." *PS: Political Science & Politics* 32(3): 583–87.

Johnson, Cedric. 2007. *Revolutionaries to Race Leaders: Black Power and the Making of African American Politics*. Minneapolis: University of Minnesota Press.

Johnson, J. H., Jr., W. C. Farrell Jr., and C. Guinn. 1997. "Immigration Reform and the Browning of America: Tensions, Conflicts, and Community Instability in Metropolitan Los Angeles." *International Migration Review* 31(4): 1055–95.

Jones, Charles E., and Michael L. Clemons. 1993. "A Model of Racial Crossover Voting." In *Dilemmas of Black Politics: Issues of Leadership and Strategy*, ed. Georgia A. Persons. New York: HarperCollins College.

Jordan, Mary, and R. H. Melton. 1988. "Dawkins Ads Hint Robb Is Untrustworthy." *Washington Post*, 14 October, C6.

Juenke, Eric Gonzalez, and Anna Sampaio. 2010. "Deracialization and Latino Politics: The Case of the Salazar Brothers in Colorado." *Political Research Quarterly* 63(1): 43–54.

Kahn K. F., and P. J. Kenney. 1999. "Do Negative Campaigns Mobilize or Suppress Turnout? Clarifying the Relationship between Negativity and Participation." *American Political Science Review* 93(4): 877–89.

Kaufmann, Karen M. 2003. "Cracks in the Rainbow: Group Commonality as a Basis for Latino and African American Political Coalitions." *Political Research Quarterly* 56(2): 199–210.

Keele, Luke, and Ismail White. 2011. "African-American Turnout in Majority-Minority Districts." Annual Meeting of the American Political Science Association.

Keen, Judy. 2006. "Websites Win Candidates' Praise; Young People Pushed Them to Get Online." *USA Today,* 17 October.

Kinder, Donald, and Lynn Sanders. 1996. *Divided by Color: Racial Politics and Democratic Ideals*. Chicago: University of Chicago Press.

King-Meadows, Tyson. 2010. "The 'Steele Problem' and the New Republican Battle for Black Votes: Legacy, Loyalty, and Lexicon in Maryland's 2006 Senate Contest. In *Whose Black Politics? Cases in Post-Racial Black Leadership*, ed. Andra Gillespie. New York: Routledge.

Krebs, Timothy, and David Holian. 2007. "Competitive Positioning, Deracialization, and Attack Speech: A Study of Negative Campaigning in the 2001 Los Angeles Mayoral Election." *American Politics Research* 35(1): 123–49.

Lewis-Beck, M. S., C. Tien, and R. Nadeau. 2009. "Obama's Missed Landslide: A Racial Cost?" *PS: Political Science & Politics* 43(1): 69–76.

Lublin, David. 1997. *The Paradox of Representation: Racial Gerrymandering and Minority Interests in Congress*. Princeton: Princeton University Press.

———. 1999. "Racial Redistricting and African American Representation: A Critique of 'Do Majority-Minority Districts Maximize Substantive Black Representation in Congress?'" *American Political Science Review* 93(1): 183–86.

Maddaus, Gene. 2008. "Ferraro Defends Controversial Comments on Barack Obama." *Daily Breeze*, 11 March. http://www.dailybreeze.com/ci_8533832

Marable, Manning. 2009. "Racializing Obama: The Enigma of Post-Black Politics and Leadership." *Souls* 11(1): 1–15.

Marelius, John. 1988. "Jackson Tells the Drug Story Like It Really Is." *San Diego Union,* 7 May, A2.

Marsh, Catherine. 1985. "Back on the Bandwagon: The Effect of Opinion Polls on Public Opinion." *British Journal of Political Science* 15(1): 51–74.

Masuoka, Natalie. 2006. "Together They Become One: Examining the Predictors of Panethnic Group Consciousness among Asian Americans and Latinos." *Social Science Quarterly* 87(5): 993–1011.

McAllister, Ian, and Donley T. Studlar. 1991. "Bandwagon, Underdog, or Projection? Opinion Polls and Electoral Choice in Britain, 1979–1987." *Journal of Politics* 53(4): 720–40.

McClain, P. D., and A. J. Karnig. 1990. "Black and Hispanic Socioeconomic and Political Composition." *American Political Science Review* 84(4): 535–45.

McClain, Paula D., Niambi M. Carter, Victoria M. DeFrancesco Soto, Monique L. Lyle, Jeffrey D. Grynaviski, Shayla C. Nunnally, Thomas J. Scotto, J. Alan Kendrick, Gerald F. Lackey, and Kendra Davenport Cotton. 2006. "Racial Distancing in a Southern City: Latino Immigrants' Views of Black Americans." *Journal of Politics* 68(3): 571–84.

McCormick, J. P., Jr., and Charles E. Jones. 1993. "The Conceptualization of Deracialization." In *Dilemmas of Black Politics*, ed. Georgia Persons, 66–84. New York: HarperCollins College.

McDermott, Monika. 1998. "Race and Gender Cues in Low Information Elections." *Political Research Quarterly* 51(4): 895–918.

McIlwain, Charlton, and Stephen Caliendo. 2011. *Race Appeal: How Candidates Invoke Race in U.S. Elections.* Philadelphia: Temple University Press.

McKee, Seth C., M. V. Hood, and David Hill. 2012. "Achieving Validation: Barack Obama and Black Turnout in 2008." *State Politics and Policy Quarterly* 12(1): 3–22.

McKenzie, Brian. 2004. "Religious Social Networks, Indirect Mobilization, and African American Political Participation." *Political Research Quarterly* 57(4): 621–32.

Mendelberg, Tali. 2001. *The Race Card: Campaign Strategy, Implicit Messages, and the Norm of Equality.* Princeton: Princeton University Press.

Metz, David H., and Katherine Tate. 1995. "The Color of Urban Campaigns." In *Classifying by Race,* ed. Paul Peterson. Princeton: Princeton University Press.

Min Baek, Young, and Jocelyn Landau. 2011. "White Concern about Black Favoritism in a Biracial Presidential Election." *American Politics Research* 39(2): 291–322.

Mitchell, Charlie. 2008. "Democrats Being Practical, Not Racist." *Enterprise-Journal,* 10 September, Opinion.

Mitchell, Mary. 2008. "Why Is Tavis Smiley Dissing Sen. Barack Obama?" *Chicago Sun-Times,* 14 February.

Mooney, Mark. 2008. "Bubba: Obama Is Just Like Jesse Jackson." *ABC News,* 26 January. http://abcnews.go.com/blogs/politics/2008/01/bubba-obama-is/.

Navarrette, Ruben, Jr. 2002. "Rainbow Politics Down in Texas." *Washington Post,* 20 October, B07.

Neff, Erin. 2002. "Race for Governor Remains Low-Key." *Las Vegas Sun,* 9 October, B1.

Nelson, Thomas E., Kira Sanbonmatsu, and Harwood K. McClerking. 2007. "Playing a Different Race Card: Examining the Limits of Elite Influence on Perceptions of Racism." *Journal of Politics* 69(2): 416–29.

Obama, Barack. 2006. *The Audacity of Hope: Thoughts on Reclaiming the American Dream.* Edinburgh: Canongate Books.

———. 2008. "A More Perfect Union." *Black Scholar* 38(1): 17–23.

O'Brien, Conor Cruise. 1988. "Jackson, Two-Way Loser: The Democrats' Dilemma." *Times,* 13 April.

Orey, Byron. 2006. "Deracialization or Racialization: The Making of a Black Mayor in Jackson, Mississippi." *Politics and Policy* 34(4): 814–36.

Orey, Bryon, and Boris Ricks. 2007. "A Systematic Analysis of the Deracialization Concept." University of Nebraska. *Faculty Publications: Political Science,* 325–34.

Peffley, Mark, and Jon Hurwitz. 2007. "Persuasion and Resistance: Race and the Death Penalty in America." *American Journal of Political Science* 51(4): 996–1012.

Perry, Huey L. 1996. *Race, Politics, and Governance in the United States.* Gainesville: University Press of Florida.

Perry, Ravi. 2011. "Kindred Political Rhetoric: Black Mayors, President Obama, and the Universalizing of Black Interests." *Journal of Urban Affairs* 33(5): 567–89.

Philpot, Tasha, Daron Shaw, and Ernest McGowen. 2009. "Winning the Race: Black Voter Turnout in the 2008 Presidential Election." *Public Opinion Quarterly* 73(5): 995–1022.

Philpot, Tasha, and Hanes Walton. 2007. "One of Our Own: Black Female Candidates and the Voters Who Support Them." *American Journal of Political Science* 51(1): 49–62.

Pickler, Nedra. 2007. "Obama Says He Can Turn Out Black Voters." *USA Today,* 21 August, A1.

Pierannunzi, Carol, and John Hutcheson. 1996. "The Rise and Fall of Deracialization: Andrew Young as Mayor and Gubernatorial Candidate." In *Race, Politics, and Governance in the United States,* ed. Huey L. Perry. Gainesville: University of Florida Press.

Piston, Spencer. 2010. "How Explicit Racial Prejudice Hurt Obama in the 2008 Election." *Political Behavior* 32(4): 431–51.

Presser, Stanley. 1990. "Can Changes in Context Reduce Vote Overreporting in Surveys?" *Public Opinion Quarterly* 54(4): 586–93.

Preston, Michael. 1983. "The Election of Harold Washington: Black Voting Patterns in the 1983 Chicago Mayoral Race." *PS: Political Science & Politics* 16(2): 486–88.

Ratcliffe, R. G. 2002. "Election 2002: Senate Candidates Spar Again." *Houston Chronicle,* 24 October.

Reeves, Keith. 1997. *Voting Hopes or Fears?* New York: Oxford University Press.

Robnett, Belinda, and Katherine Tate. 2012. "UCI Outlook on Life and Political Engagement," 31 December.

Rosenstone, Steven J., and John Mark Hansen. 1993. *Mobilization, Participation, and Democracy in America.* New York: Macmillan.

Ross, Brian. 2008. "Obama's Pastor: God Damn America, U.S. to Blame for 9/11." *ABC News,* 13 March. http://abcnews.go.com/Blotter/DemocraticDebate/story?id =4443788HYPERLINK "http://abcnews.go.com/Blotter/DemocraticDebate/story ?id=4443788&page=1"&HYPERLINK "http://abcnews.go.com/Blotter/Democratic Debate/story?id=4443788&page=1"page=1#.T6BfGavY98E.

Royko, Mike. 1988. "Plague of the Primaries Is Gone from Illinois." *Orange County Register,* 18 March, J12.

Schelzig, Erik. 2006a. "Obama Urges Tenn. Voters to Make Ford First Black Senator from South in More than 100 Years." Associated Press, 6 November.

———. 2006b. "Ford Tries to Energize Black Vote in West Tennessee." Associated Press, 30 October.

Schildkraut, Deborah J. 2005. "The Rise and Fall of Political Engagement among Latinos: The Role of Identity and Perceptions of Discrimination." *Political Behavior* 27(3): 285–312.

Schmich, Mary T. "Young Loses Governor Runoff: Democrats Nominate Moderate Miller in Georgia." *Chicago Tribune*, 8 August 1990.

Scoppe, Cindi Ross. 1990. "Campbell Backers Sold Out Blacks, Mitchell Charges." *State*, 26 September, 1A.

Secret, Phillip, James Johnson, and Audrey Forrest. 1990. "The Impact of Religiosity on Political Participation and Membership in Voluntary Associations among Black and White Americans." *Journal of Black Politics* 21(1): 87–102.

Serwer, Adam. 2008. "He's Black, Get Over It." The American Prospect http://prospect.org/article/hes-black-get-over-it. Accessed on 5 June 2012.

Shaughnessy, Rick. 1986. "Jackson Backs Chacon Race Issue Raised." *San Diego Union Tribune*, 14 October, A4.

Sher, Andy. 2008. "State GOP Backs Off Statement on Obama; Republicans Withdraw Web Site Release Using Democrat's Middle Name." *Chattanooga Times Free Press*, 28 February, 1.

Sigelman, Carol, Lee Sigelman, Barbara Walkosz, and Michael Nitz. 1995. "Black Candidates, White Voters: Understanding Racial Bias in Political Perceptions." *American Journal of Political Science* 39(1): 243–65.

Sigelman, Lee, and James S. Todd. 1992. "Clarence Thomas, Black Pluralism, and Civil Rights Policy." *Political Science Quarterly* 107 (2): 231–48.

Sigelman, Lee, and Susan Welch. 1994. *Black Americans' Views of Racial Inequality: The Dream Deferred.* New York: Cambridge University Press.

Silver, Brian D., Barbara A. Anderson, and Paul R. Abramson. 1986. "Who Overreports Voting?" *American Political Science Review* 80(2): 613–24.

Skocpol, Theda. 1991. "Targeting within Universalism: Politically Viable Policies to Combat Poverty in the United States." In *The Urban Underclass,* ed. Christopher Jencks and Paul E. Peterson. Washington, D.C.: Brookings Institution.

Smith, Robert C. 1990. "Recent Elections and Black Politics: The Maturation or Death of Black Politics." *PS: Political Science & Politics* 23(2): 160–62.

Sniderman, Paul M., and Edward H. Stiglitz. 2008. "Race and the Moral Character of the Modern American Experience." *Forum* 6(4).

Sonenshein, R. J. 1990. "Can Black Candidates Win Statewide Elections?" *Political Science Quarterly* 105(2): 219–41.

Spence, Lester K., and Harwood McClerking. 2010. "Context, Black Empowerment, and African American Political Participation." *American Politics Research* 38(5): 909–30.

Stout, Christopher T. 2010. "Black Empowerment in the Age of Obama." PhD diss., University of California, Irvine.

Stout, Christopher T., and Danvy Le. 2012. "Living the Dream: Barack Obama and Blacks' Changing Perceptions of the American Dream." *Social Science Quarterly* 93(5): 1338–59.

Strickland, Ruth Ann, and Marcia Lynn Whicker. 1992. "Comparing the Wilder and Gantt Campaigns: A Model for Black Candidate Success in Statewide Elections." *PS: Political Science & Politics* 25(2): 204–12.

Strong, Tom. 1990. "Mitchell's Gubernatorial Dream Seems to Be Fading." *Charlotte Observer*, 29 October, 1N.

Summers, Mary, and Philip Klinkner. 1990. "The Election of John Daniels as Mayor of New Haven." *PS: Political Science & Politics* 23(2): 142–45.

———. 1996. "The Election and Governance of John Daniels as Mayor of New Haven and the Failure of the Deracialization Hypothesis." In *Race, Politics, and Governance in the United States*, ed. Huey L. Perry. Gainesville: University Press of Florida.

Surratt, Clark. 1990. "Unrepentant Mitchell Goes on the Offensive." *State*, 3 October, 1A.

Susswein, Gary. 2002. "Rivals Clash over Ties to Business; Kirk, Cornyn Have Testy Exchange on Issues and Each Other's Links to Enron." *Austin American-Statesman*, 19 October, 1.

Swain, Carol. 1993. *Black Faces, Black Interests*. Cambridge: Harvard University Press.

Sweet, Lynn. 1992. "A Critical Analysis of Campaign Ads." *Chicago Sun-Times*, 29 October 29, A5.

Tate, Katherine. 1991. "Black Political Participation in the 1984 and 1988 Presidential Elections." *American Political Science Review* 85(4): 1159–76.

———. 1993. *From Protest to Politics: The New Black Voters in American Elections*. Cambridge: Harvard University Press.

———. 2003. *Black Faces in the Mirror: African Americans and Their Representatives in the U.S. Congress*. Princeton: Princeton University Press.

———. 2010. *What's Going On? Political Incorporation and the Transformation of Black Public Opinion*. Washington, D.C.: Georgetown University Press.

———. 2012. "Black Power in Black Presidential Politics from Jackson to Obama." *National Political Science Review* 13(1): 13–18

Taylor, Joe. 1988. "Robb's All-American Image Bruised by Battle for Senate in Virginia." Associated Press, 29 October.

Terkildsen, Nayda. 1993. "When White Voters Evaluate Black Candidates: The Processing Implications of Candidate Skin Color, Prejudice, and Self-Monitoring." *American Journal of Political Science* 37(3): 1032–53.

Terkildsen, Nayda, and David F. Damore. 1999. "The Dynamic of Racialized Media Coverage in Congressional Elections." *Journal of Politics* 61(3): 680–99.

Uhlaner, Carole. 1989a. "Rational Turnout: The Neglected Role of Groups." *American Journal of Political Science* 33(2): 390–422.

———. 1989b. "'Relational Goods' and Participation: Incorporating Sociability into a Theory of Rational Action." *Public Choice* 62(3): 253–85.

Vaca, Nick Corona. 2004. *The Presumed Alliance: The Unspoken Conflict between Latinos and Blacks and What It Means for America*. St. Louis: San Val.

Valentino, Nicholas A., Vincent L. Hutchings, and Ismail K. White. 2002. "Cues That Matter: How Political Ads Prime Racial Attitudes during Campaigns." *American Political Science Review* 96(1): 75–90.

Vanderleeuw, James, Baodong Liu, and Greg Marsh. 2004. "Applying Black Threat Theory, Urban Regime Theory, and Deracialization: The Memphis Mayoral Elections of 1991, 1995, and 1999." *Journal of Urban Affairs* 26(4): 505–19.

Vogel, Ed. 2002. "Guinn Awaits Neal in Governor." *Las Vegas Review-Journal*, 4 September, 5A.

Walker, Clarence E., and Gregory D. Smithers. 2009. *The Preacher and the Politician: Jeremiah Wright, Barack Obama, and Race in America.* Charlottesville: University of Virginia Press.

Walker, Tony. 2008. "In a Recession on the Wrong Track; The Polls–U.S. Economy." *Australian Financial Review*, 2 May.

Walters, Ronald W. 2007. "Barack Obama and the Politics of Blackness." *Journal of Black Politics* 38(1): 7–29.

Washington, Ebonya. 2006. "How Black Candidates Affect Voter Turnout." *Quarterly Journal of Economics* 121(3): 973–88.

Weaver, Vesla M. 2012. "The Electoral Consequences of Skin Color: The 'Hidden' Side of Race in Politics." *Political Behavior* 34(1): 159–92.

White, Ismail. 2007. "When Race Matters and When It Doesn't: Racial Group Differences in Response to Racial Cues." *American Political Science Review* 101(2): 339–54.

Williams, Huntington. 1990. "Taking Helms by the Tarheel." *Washington Post*, 21 October, C1.

Wilson, William J. 1980. *The Declining Significance of Race.* Chicago: University of Chicago Press.

Wright, Sharon. 1996. "The Deracialization Strategy and African American Candidates in Memphis Mayoral Elections." In *Race, Politics, and Governance in the United States*, ed. Huey L. Perry, 151–64. Gainesville: University Press of Florida.

Younge, Gary. 2007. "The Obama Effect." *Nation*, 13 December. http://www.thenation.com/article/obama-effect.

Zeleny, Jeff. 2010. "Alabama Candidate Tries Obama Coalition Style." *New York Times*, 31 May, A14.

Zeleny, Jeff, and Carl Hulse. 2008. "Kennedy Chooses Obama, Spurning Plea by Clinton." *New York Times*, 28 January.

Index

RACE, ETHNICITY, AND POLITICS